INVESTING IN
REAL ESTATE
PRIVATE
EQUITY

An Insider's Guide to Real Estate Partnerships,
Funds, Joint Ventures & Crowdfunding

Sean Cook

For my boys, particularly the one who asked if he could meet our investment minimums by collecting subscriptions from his second-grade classmates.

CONTENTS

Preface 1

Glossary 8

Chapter 1: Investment Structures 12

Chapter 2: Evaluating Deals - Products, Strategies, & Capital Structures 42

      Office 43

      Retail 44

      Industrial 45

      Multifamily 46

      Other/Specialty Products 47

      NNN (Triple Net) 48

      Land Investments 48

      Tangible Stuff: Sticks & Bricks 50

      Location 53

      Positioning in the Marketplace 53

      Tenants & Investment Strategy 55

      A) All Cash / All Equity 58

      B) Debt 59

      C) Subordinate Debt 67

      D) Preferred Equity 69

      Evaluating the Capital Structure 71

Chapter 3: Evaluating the Sponsor 73

Chapter 4: Compensation & Fees 78

      Investor Classes 92

Chapter 5: Joint Ventures & Exchange/TIC Considerations 99

GP Co-invest & Compensation 100

Major Decisions & Removal Rights 100

Financing & Recourse 101

Buy/Sell 102

Timing & Process 103

Major Investors 103

Chapter 6: Modeling, Valuations, & Return Projections 106

Comparable Sales 107

Replacement Cost 108

Discounted Cash Flow (DCF) or Income Capitalization Approach 112

Chapter 7: Metrics, Ratios, & Quantitative Miscellany 118

Multiples 118

Cap Rates 120

Cash on Cash Returns 122

Current Return 123

Risk Metrics 123

Revenue Stress Test 123

Loan-to-value (LTV) 126

DCR & Debt Yield 127

Chapter 8: Market Forecasts & Economic Storytelling 129

Chapter 9: Crafting & Executing Your Strategy 136

Setting an Allocation 136

Investment Strategy & Risk Profile 139

Finding and Reviewing Offerings 144

Defining Your Investment Strategy (Picking Your Poison) 145

Real Estate Market Efficiency 148

Identifying and Evaluating Managers 150

Chapter 10: Pulling the Trigger: Investment Process & Timeline 161

Private Placement Memorandum (PPM) 163

Limited Partnership Agreement or Operating Agreement 164

Other Transaction Materials 164

Subscription Agreement 165

Review and Commitment 166

Chapter 11: Key Takeaways 167

Postscript 168

References 170

PREFACE

"My father was very sure about certain matters pertaining to the universe. To him, all good things – trout as well as eternal salvation – come by grace and grace comes by art and art does not come easy." – A river runs through it – Norman MacLean

When the time came to inform investors of the impending calamity, I sat down under the plasma TV on the maple credenza at the end of the long conference room. It was standing room only, packed with employees, many of whom had as much or more at stake than our investors. Eyes were trained on the carpet rather than the black conference phone, which was filled with investors and sat alone in the middle of the conference table. No notes were taken, no blackberries checked, no weekend plans discussed. The only voice was the chairman's, as he explained reality to the phone, and by extension to the rest of the room. Thus commenced the formerly venerable company's slow motion implosion; a series of events that took it from the front page of the Wall Street Journal to a footnote in the resumes of former employees and a capital loss on the tax returns of its investors. Thus also commenced my true appreciation of the complexity of the real estate business.

Good times also abound in the real estate business of course. While that odious moment on the credenza will remain forever in my memory, there are plenty of pleasant memories to accompany it. Great colleagues, fantastic investments, putting contests in the hallway, introvert-torturing conferences, late nights of proofreading, many trips on Southwest Airlines, and the gratification of watching properties' slow motion transformation into something more beautiful for residents, tenants, and their neighborhoods. The real estate investment business is an endlessly fascinating and addictive pastime, which is probably why it has such broad appeal.

1

As an industry participant, I'm often asked to opine on deals in which friends or acquaintances are considering an investment. Going through other companies' offerings is entertaining market research and helpful as I think about the appeal of my deals to potential investors. I try to offer my candid opinions, which are sometimes positive and sometimes less so. Like many real estate investors, my friends are real estate hobbyists; experts in other more useful industries. They look to real estate to generate some additional income, diversify their existing investment portfolio, and for some entertainment (although few like to admit it). I started looking for a simple resource or book that I could recommend to provide some more general guidance about how to make these investments. Surprisingly, despite the size of the private equity real estate industry, I struggled to find a good handbook for investors in private partnerships and funds. Many resources are mind-numbingly boring, overly technical, or focused on making direct real estate investments; a strategy I don't think is advisable for most non-professional investors. The impetus of this book is to provide readers with this summary of the basic tools needed to evaluate and make private real estate investments. Along the way, I share some personal observations about the actual mechanics of the industry along with a few thoughts on more active joint-venture arrangements, crowdfunding, and other special cases. I hope this provides a practical summary of the real estate investment business and a solid framework to create and execute your own unique real estate investment strategy whether you are a property neophyte or a seasoned expert.

There is a common misconception that the way to make money in real estate is by doing it yourself. Consider the blizzard of purportedly educational books and courses on real estate. Most of them are get-rich-quick gimmicks trying to sell a dream of flipping houses with no money down or building a commercial real estate empire from scratch. Go ahead – type "real estate investment" or something similar into your favorite search engine and see what comes up. Sleaze!

I'm not sure what it is about the real estate industry that causes people to shy away from hiring professionals. In this case, "hiring a professional" means investing through companies who specialize in a real estate strategy and earn a fee for their services. Would you build your own toaster? Write your own operating system? Perform your own root canal? We embrace specialization nearly everywhere else in our economy and real estate need be no different.

Can you make millions in real estate without expertise? Perhaps, but you can lose it too. Unfortunately, there have been enough real estate entrepreneurs who bootstrapped their way to success to make the dream appear almost within reach, but the reality for most first-time investors is harsh. The invest-for-yourself hucksters do the industry a disservice by convincing people to take enormous risk in a competitive business where they have minimal expertise. This is a recipe for disaster, and it has fostered an environment where too many people who have recognized the legitimate benefits of a private real estate investment allocation try to go it alone and end up losing money and many nights of sleep for avoidable reasons.

If you are looking for a get-rich-quick book telling you how to put no money down and deal-flip your way to millions in riches, or if you want a magic recipe for real estate investing that can't lose, save yourself some time and look elsewhere – this is not the book for you. Although for some large and experienced investors it makes sense to source, purchase, improve, and manage their own real estate investment portfolio, the majority of investors would be better served by the more passive and diversified approach discussed herein.

Here's why:

- Regardless of what many scam artists will have you believe; real estate is a complicated and nuanced business that takes years of experience and painful lessons learned before you begin to not suck. You might spend a lifetime pursuing mastery of a single asset class, let alone the entire industry. Being 95% expert is not enough. Little oversights can cost big money.

- Specialist operators cover every potential transaction within their area of expertise and have the market knowledge to identify and execute on only what they deem to be the best opportunities. Logical evaluation is not enough to make good investment decisions. Commercial real estate can be very illiquid, so this market knowledge and historical context is necessary to understand how an opportunity prices in comparison with the rest of the market. The process of tracking and bidding on comps is critical to being able to "buy right".

• A failed transaction can cost sellers significant money, so a strong industry reputation is critical to both controlling deals and getting an attractive price. This credibility takes years to build through successful transactions and ongoing industry relationships. Without it, the only way to get deals is to over-pay.

• Operating commercial real estate, like any business, isn't all (or even mostly) glamor. The daily reality is a time sucking, thankless endeavor. If you have a day job or are enjoying your retirement, think twice before taking on a project that can involve phone calls at all hours of the day and night. On the other hand, if you're bored and looking for a hobby to entertain yourself or a second career, perhaps this is just what you're looking for!

• Property management and investment operations are significantly improved (or simply more efficient) when done with scale. Few private owners have the wherewithal to build a diversified portfolio with enough scale to be truly efficient and large enough to benefit from negotiating power in the industry.

This book is an attempt to deviate from the get-rich-quick norm. You don't need to directly buy your own property to be an owner and reap the benefits of an investment allocation to real estate. My goal is to create a simple and practical field guide describing how to create a real estate portfolio by investing with private operators. This type of investment is known as "private real estate" or "private equity real estate", as opposed to investments commonly made in publicly traded real estate companies (usually real estate investment trusts - REITs). Think of this as making an investment in a small privately owned company or in a venture capital fund rather than by buying stock or mutual funds through your investment broker. This book is about partnering or investing with operators who have specific expertise in their niche, allowing you to actively manage the type of real estate you invest in (even individually pick properties), without doing it all yourself. You won't learn how to evaluate, buy, and manage your own properties here. Rather, we explore how to find the most experienced operators in the spaces that interest you and partner with them – let them use their lessons learned, operational platform, relationships, and reputation to your advantage.

If you feel like this approach means taking the easy way out, or you are needlessly paying fees for something you could do yourself... don't. This is the strategy many of the world's most sophisticated investors take, including multi-billion-dollar pension funds and other institutional investors. Even industry insiders (operators, brokers, attorneys, etc.) commonly invest with their peers in sectors outside their personal expertise.

Until recently, private equity real estate investments were limited by law to high-net-worth investors who met certain accreditation (wealth and income) requirements. Legislative changes have opened these investments to nearly everyone, bringing flocks of new investors to the private real estate industry through crowdfunding companies that market private real estate investments online. Whether you are a professional institutional investor or just dabbling in crowdfunded deals, we will discuss how to use the same approaches to evaluate investments and build your real estate portfolio.

This book will cover:

- What a private real estate investment is
- Fundamentals for basic real estate evaluation
- How to evaluate operators and investments
- Fees, incentives, and other loads
- Common terms and structures
- Strategies to evaluate and manage risk
- How to create and execute a personalized investment strategy

Most of this book is about the mechanics of investing and the practical aspects of sourcing, reviewing, and participating in private offerings. But investing in others' offerings doesn't mean you can't have an opinion on market trends and create a unique portfolio of assets tailored specifically to your needs and preferences. Rather than spending your time reading leases, you can spend your time on the more entertaining and gratifying task of creating a unique investment strategy.

One of the difficulties with a book like this is the lack of industry standardization. The breadth and variety of investment structures and terms available to investors is dizzying. Each offering, even those from the same manager, has its own unique nuances. Nevertheless, there are some commonalities between most private offerings. Rather than note every exception and variation, I try to focus on the most common structures and situations with a few special cases, and spend time on more generally describing how the business works so you can evaluate for yourself the inevitably unique offerings coming your way.

You might as well note upfront my decision to write under a pseudonym. The investment industry strongly encourages participants to be stuffily professional; buttoned down, tucked in, slicked back, and generally Confidence Inspiring. As an active member of the real estate industry, I want to avoid creating another generic marketing fluff piece. My goal here is not to convince you to buy something or to invest in something. I'm not trying to sell you anything (except this book, obviously). This is just an anonymous chat about real estate, o.k.? Invest with whomever you want. My identity is therefore unnecessary, in fact counterproductive, in trying to share my candid thoughts, experiences, and occasionally heterodox opinions about the industry. Anonymity saves both of us from the need to pretend this whole endeavor is more than it is. Don't take this the wrong way; I take my responsibility as an investor extremely seriously, doing my very best to craft the finest investments that market conditions will allow. In fact, it's this goal of crafting truly good investments that leads me to question the precision of our models, the accuracy of our market forecasts, and the complexity of our capital structures – unpopular topics in the insular investment world. Understanding the reality of the real estate industry is a prerequisite to using its products effectively.

For those interested in my background, if only for context, here are some basics: I have an undergraduate engineering degree and an MBA in finance. I'm young enough to use the word "like" unintentionally, but old enough to be aggravated by this unfortunate tendency. After a few years of engineering work in the aerospace industry I switched to the finance side of the business because venture capital and M&A seemed like fun. I liked deal making but not large company life, so I followed some business school friends to a commercial real estate mortgage banking company to learn the business. I worked for a multi-billion dollar family office evaluating investments (giving me an appreciation for the difficulty of evaluating offerings), as well as for a start-up distressed-mortgage hedge fund (giving me an appreciation for the difficulty of starting a company). The majority of my real estate experience has been on the owner/operator side; buying property, putting together offerings, and interfacing with our investors. My experience includes over $1 billion in transactions and spans the major property types, with a strong focus on, and affinity for, multifamily. As a result, many of the examples herein tend to relate to multifamily but are usually generalizable to other product types.

I encourage you not to take advice from anyone because of their title or experience, and I hope my ideas will stand on their own merit. I'm not an attorney or a financial adviser, so look elsewhere for legal or investment advice. My goal here is to share my insider's knowledge about real estate private equity to help investors allocate capital more effectively to private real estate. Take my opinions for what they are and abide them, or not, as you see fit. As the Kalama Sutta says, "When you know for yourselves that, these qualities are skillful; these qualities are blameless; these qualities are praised by the wise; these qualities, when adopted & carried out, lead to welfare & to happiness, then you should enter & remain in them." The real estate investment world is full of advice and I sincerely hope you find at least some of mine useful. It is up to you to form your own conclusions and choose your own path. I hope your path leads you to wealth, manageable levels of stress, and perhaps some entertainment along the way.

Ok, enough chit-chat. Let's get this show on the road!

GLOSSARY

Real estate, like any specialized pursuit, involves a lot of acronyms and terms of art. I try to avoid being unnecessarily technical in this book, mostly because unlike other specialized pursuits, real estate isn't actually all that complicated. While real estate analysis can be intricate, as we will discuss later, sometimes the simplest analyses are the most robust. The complicated stuff… some of it is useful but a lot is just storytelling. A few acronyms and specific terms just can't be escaped. It's important to know the basics so you really understand the investment you're considering.

I realize glossaries are usually in the back of books, but I'm going to ignore that particular convention. What's the point of waiting until the end for all this juicy content? Just skim it, then flip back to this section as a quick reference as you read. Or skip to Chapter 1 if you're a traditionalist. These concepts are described in much more detail later in the book so don't worry if this quick explanation doesn't seem sufficient; it's just for reference.

Cap Rate: A measure of the income generated without debt, from an investment in real estate. A deal's cap rate is its NOI (Net Operating Income) divided by the property's purchase price. Higher is often better, but there are plenty of complexities to this, which we address later. The cap rate in real estate is used in a similar way as the Price/Earnings ratio in corporate investments except it's flipped upside down… can't make things too easy!

Carried Interest: An incentive compensation structure where the sponsor of a real estate investment receives a portion of the profits if the deal goes well. Carried interest, or "carry" is also referred to as a "promote".

Crowdfunding: The practice of raising money openly from investors, usually through a web-based portal. This is a relatively new, but rapidly growing, strategy made possible through legislation passed in 2012. Many crowdfunded deals are structurally like, or made in combination with, traditional private real estate offerings.

DCR (Debt Coverage Ratio) or DSCR (Debt Service Coverage Ratio): A factor frequently considered by lenders when determining how risky a loan is. It is also useful for equity investors – if lenders are nervous about a deal, equity investors should be terrified. The DCR is a property's net operating income (NOI) divided by the debt service payment.

Cash-on-Cash Return: The annual cash dividend from operations distributed to investors, divided by the initial cash investment in the deal. It is sort of like the yield on a bond or the annual dividend from a stock.

Fund: An investment vehicle where a sponsor buys, operates, and sells multiple properties on behalf of multiple passive investors.

GP (General Partner): The sponsor of a transaction structured as a Limited Partnership.

Investment Multiple: A ratio defined as all the money you get out of a deal (from operations or from disposition), divided by your investment in the deal. The bigger the better... obviously. Unlike other measures of investment returns, investment multiples are agnostic about how long your money is tied up in a deal.

IRR (Internal Rate of Return): The compounded annual return on an investment. The IRR incorporates all cash flows into or out of an investment, including the initial investment, operational distributions, and proceeds from the sale or refinancing of a property. Bigger is better when it comes to IRRs, but beware of temptingly high investment projections resulting from unreasonably optimistic assumptions.

JV (Joint Venture): A real estate transaction made with one passive investor and one sponsor.

LLC (Limited Liability Company): A commonly used type of legal entity created to invest in real estate and shield the underlying investors from some types of liability.

LP (Limited Partnership): Like an LLC, this is another commonly used type of legal entity created to invest in real estate and shield the underlying investors from some types of liability. The acronyms "LP" or "LPs" could be referring to either the legal entities or to the underlying passive investors; readers are left to figure this out based on context.

LP (Limited Partner): A passive investor in a real estate deal. This term is specific to investors in a Limited Partnership entity. As described above, the acronyms "LP" or "LPs" could be referring to either the legal entities or to the underlying passive investors.

LPA (Limited Partnership Agreement): The legal document governing the mechanics of how a specific limited partnership entity will operate.

LTV (Loan to Value Ratio): Another measure commonly used by lenders and equity investors as a measure of risk. The LTV is the loan amount divided by the value of the property. The higher the LTV, the higher the leverage used in the transaction, and the riskier the deal. "Value", as we discuss later, could mean any one of a number of things, somewhat limiting the usefulness of this metric.

Manager or Managing Member: The sponsor of a transaction structured as a Limited Liability Company.

Member: A passive investor in a real estate deal. This term is specific to investors in an LLC (Limited Liability Company) entity.

Multiple: See "Investment Multiple"

NOI (Net Operating Income): A measure of the profitability of a property. NOI is the cash flow available from property operations after all normal revenue and expenses are accounted for, but before debt service and extraordinary expenses are paid for. Sort of the real estate version of EBITDA.

NPV (Net Present Value): A measure of the risk-adjusted profitability of an investment. Defined as the value of all cash flows (in and out of a deal) after they have been discounted correctly to today's value. Somewhat uncommon outside of the classroom. The IRR is usually used in real estate instead to describe investment returns.

Operating Agreement: The legal document governing the mechanics of how a specific limited liability company entity will operate.

Operator: A sponsor (someone who puts deals together for passive investors) who also handles day-to-day operations at a property such as on-site management or construction management. Operators are usually larger, vertically integrated investment companies.

PPM (Private Placement Memorandum): A document summarizing everything important about an investment opportunity; a summary of the real estate, plans for operating and improving the property, information about the

Glossary

GP/manager, a description of the economics of the investment, and other key information. Investors should read this, even if it's boring as hell. You'll almost always find something unexpected and important in here that you should know before you sink your hard-earned savings into a deal.

Pref (Preferred Return): The investment return rate that passive investors must receive before the sponsor begins to earn carried interest. Could be either compounded or non-compounded.

Promote: See "Carried Interest"

REIT (Real Estate Investment Trust): A specific type of pooled real estate investment vehicle, the most well-known of which are traded publicly on exchanges like stocks.

Sponsor: A generic term used to describe a GP (General Partner) or manager in a situation where the type of entity is indeterminate. This is the person, people, or company in charge of putting together a real estate investment and dealing with ongoing operations after it is purchased. While this term is commonly used in the industry, I find it confusingly similar to the term "plan sponsor", which often refers to the managers of pension plans; a very different business from being a real estate syndicate sponsor.

Subscription Agreement: A form to be completed and returned when you decide to commit to invest in a property or fund. This describes how the investment will be legally vested and usually includes a representation that you have read the offering documents and are sophisticated enough to be allowed to invest in the offering.

Syndication or Syndicate: A single real estate transaction made with multiple passive investors and one sponsor.

Waterfall: A description of how cash distributions from operations or the sale of a property will be made. Sponsor incentive compensation structures and non-standard capital structures (such as preferred equity) are often apparent when reviewing a transaction's waterfall in offering documents.

CHAPTER 1: INVESTMENT STRUCTURES

"Shares are not mere pieces of paper. They represent part ownership of a business. So, when contemplating an investment, think like a prospective owner." – Warren Buffet

Since you're still reading, let's operate from the not unreasonable assumption that you are interested in investing in real estate. You recognize the value of an allocation to real estate in your otherwise well diversified portfolio and are now deciding how to invest your allocation. Of course, you can simply go out and buy property directly, but I suggest that this might not be the most efficient strategy for most investors. Pooling your investment with others allows you to spread your real estate allocation across more properties (lowering concentration risk) and take advantage of the expertise of professional investors. Real estate needs to be owned and managed by someone though, so a number of legal structures have emerged to allow investors to work together to buy real estate, while still allowing for efficient decisions to be made on behalf of many underlying owners.

In this chapter, we discuss common structures for pooled real estate investments as well as some of the benefits and drawbacks of each. When you hand over your hard-earned money, you should know exactly what you are getting in return. It is ultimately up to you to determine which of these structures (or combination thereof) makes the most sense given your individual situation.

As with any investment, there are a variety of factors that should be considered. Before picking a product type, here is a short set of questions to ask yourself:

- How much money, in total, do you want to allocate to real estate? Within this allocation, how much diversification do you want?
- Are you comfortable trusting someone else to make investments or do you want to pick individual properties? Would you prefer to have an active strategy of picking properties or to have a passively managed and broadly diversified portfolio?
- How much risk are you comfortable with? Can you withstand the total loss of an investment? An allocation?
- Do you already have exposure to real estate through another asset (mutual funds, equity in your home, a rental property, etc.) or is your income or career tied in some way to the real estate industry?
- What is your need for liquidity? How long can you tolerate your money being tied up in a property and unavailable for other investments or needs?

There are no right or wrong answers to these questions. Keep in mind the Greek aphorism to "know thyself" and consider these factors as we describe the pros and cons of each structure below.

Public REITs

This is a book about private real estate, but publicly traded REITs need to at least be discussed briefly as a common and efficient way to allocate money to real estate. Before we discuss alternatives, let's pause briefly to talk about the REIT class and how it could fit in to your strategy. The REIT structure was created by the U.S. Congress in 1960 to enable a real estate version of the mutual fund. REITs are companies that own a portfolio of real estate (equity REITs) or mortgages (mortgage REITs). At least 90% of the income from this portfolio is then distributed directly to shareholders, who then pay taxes on that income. Many REITs are publicly traded on major stock exchanges, which means real estate ownership could be just a few clicks away via your online brokerage account. Liquidating your real estate investment is just as easy. This liquidity is perhaps the most important attribute that differentiates REITs from private real estate investments.

In general, equity REITs tend to hold higher quality properties, in better locations, for longer periods of time, than most private real estate funds or operators. REITs tend to be large (average market cap is $4 billion (NAREIT n.d.)) because there are significant one-time and ongoing regulatory costs associated with operating a publicly traded company and raising debt and equity from public markets, and these costs need to be spread over a large portfolio to be efficient. Because of their scale, REITs need to focus on larger transactions to keep their organizations efficient, and often use lower leverage when purchasing property. The combination of large portfolios and lower leverage means that a complete meltdown of your investment is less likely. Of course, each REIT has its own investment strategy and niche, so it is impossible to generalize across the industry, but those attributes are typical.

REITs are cost effective, liquid, and tend to have high quality properties – what's not to like? A few things. First, although REITs are more tax efficient than other publicly traded corporate structures, they can't take advantage of some of the potential benefits of privately held real estate investments which we will discuss shortly.

Because they have such large and diverse portfolios, REITs tend to be lightly staffed relative to their assets under management. This has the benefit of efficiency, but can result in losing sight of operational details, creating opportunities for more astute operators to add value. Also, because they focus on larger assets, they often miss out on better priced properties because they are too small to be efficiently purchased and operated.

Although they can provide diversification to a stock portfolio (NAREIT n.d.), REITs are priced by the market and can be quite volatile. In times of market distress, they can be subject to the whims of investors and may trade at significant discounts to the value of the underlying real estate as measured by recent sales comps. This is one of the most common objections to the asset class, but I view it as more of a feature than a drawback. Just because private real estate investment values aren't marked to market daily doesn't necessarily mean the value of the real estate isn't changing; only that there is no way to know values as timely and precisely as you can with a REIT investment. Not being informed of volatility doesn't make it any less real.

Truly long-term investors who view REITs as mispriced always have the option to not sell and wait for the price to correct. Investors in a private deal simply don't have the option to sell and are forced to hold for the long term. Although illiquidity can be a drawback, it can also be a benefit depending on your investing personality – illiquid investments may save you from yourself. They can force you to hold investments for the long term when you wouldn't otherwise have the discipline to ride the market out. "Private real estate; saving investors from themselves." Not the catchiest sales pitch, which is probably why you don't hear it, but it might just be true.

Not all REITs are publicly traded, there are also public non-traded REITs and private REITs. These typically fee-heavy companies are sold by brokers who often earn 5% to 10% commissions on selling the securities. Furthermore, these companies don't benefit from the same liquidity as their publicly traded brethren. I would just skip this class of investment, but feel free to do your homework and draw your own conclusion.

For more detailed information about REITs, a very comprehensive (if biased) source of industry information is at the website for the National Association of Real Estate Investment Trusts (NAREIT – www.reit.com). This is a great resource for understanding the REIT universe and has excellent historical information.

For an even more cost effective and diversified solution than investing directly in REITs, you can simply buy shares in a low cost REIT index mutual fund such as Vanguard's VGSIX (www.vanguard.com). If you want to take this route, resources such as Morningstar (www.morningstar.com) provide a wealth of analysis about fund track records, fees, management, and other factors to help you decide from the incredible array of options.

This is a book about private real estate so information provided here about REITs is very limited, but understanding the relative benefits and drawbacks of REITs is critical to defining your overall real estate strategy so some time needs to be devoted to them. Getting real estate exposure through REITs can be cost effective, liquid, and diversified. If you have a relatively small total allocation to real estate or need the liquidity, you should absolutely be considering REITs as your simplest solution.

Syndications

Syndication is the classic method for raising money for large-scale real estate investments in which a group of investors combine their capital to purchase a single property. A single person or company organizes the syndicate and manages the investment on the investors' behalf. This strong manager role minimizes the chance that disagreements between investors might paralyze a property, damaging the value and resulting in all investors being worse off. The first large-scale syndicated transaction occurred in the 1920s, when Fred French solicited investments through the newspaper to build a residential development in Midtown Manhattan. Through the "French Plan", investors became shareholders in a corporation and received a 6% return, before splitting subsequent distributions 50/50 with French. (Goodwin Procter 2014) Not the best economic terms for investors, but there wasn't much competition at the time!

Syndications have evolved over the years, but they generally follow this script: A syndicator controls (or "ties up") a property, which usually means they have signed a purchase contract or have an option to purchase it. Then he or she performs due diligence on the property to make sure the initial investment assumptions are reasonable. During this time the syndicator arranges a mortgage and raises equity from a group of private investors. When all the pieces are in place, the property is purchased and the syndicator operates the property on behalf of the investors. Distributions are made to investors based on their ownership percentage in the entity, with the syndicator receiving additional fees and a carried interest (or "promote") bonus if the investment goes well.

Before going further, let's go through an admittedly simplistic summary of the legal mechanics of a syndicated transaction. This is pretty tedious but bear with me because these structures, or a variation on them, are used for almost all private real estate deals. Some of this will no doubt be review for experienced investors but don't worry, it won't take long. The goal of these legal structures is to shield investors from potential liability created by ownership of the property. As an investor, you might be willing to roll the dice with the money you invest in a deal, but you want your risk to stop there. You don't want a freak accident at the property or a management screw-up to result in a lawsuit costing you your entire net worth. Most syndications achieve this by forming either a limited partnership ("LP") or a limited liability company ("LLC") to own the real estate on behalf of the individual investors and to shield them from some liability. LPs and LLCs are types of legal entities; a standalone thing (company, association, partnership, etc.) that has legal capacity to sign contracts, own property, sue (and be sued), and accept legal responsibility for its actions. Single purpose entities ("SPEs") are just entities that are formed and operated to own a single property. SPEs are often required to avoid risk from common ownership; that liability from one property could impact the value of another property.

Let's start by discussing the limited partnership structure. The partnership is managed by a general partner who acts as the point of contact and makes day-to-day decisions on behalf of the partnership. Investors contribute cash to the partnership in exchange for interest in the entity as limited partners. When buying real estate, the partnership becomes the direct owner of the property and is the borrower for the mortgage. Cash from operations or the sale of a property flow through the partnership to the general partner and limited partners (we will discuss this in more detail later). When bad things happen, the general partner bears liability for the partnership and limited partners are mostly shielded from liability. A diagram of a simple limited partnership follows.

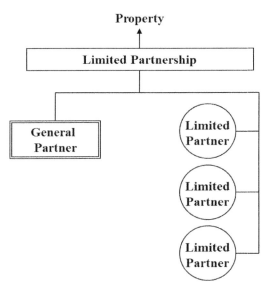

Simple Limited Partnership Structure

Generally speaking, limited liability companies operate in much the same way as LPs, but some of the names are different. The LLC owns the real estate, a managing member (or non-member manager if they have no ownership in the entity but are responsible for making decisions) makes decisions for the LLC, and the passive investors are simply members. If the prior limited partnership example were instead structured as an LLC, it would look like the following:

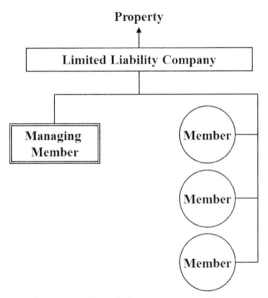

Simple Limited Liability Company Structure

Real estate companies then use one or more entities to run their transactions and to absorb liability for their business. In practice, there are a confusing variety of terms used to describe the person, people, or company in charge of putting deals together and making decisions on behalf of passive investors. For the sake of clarity, in this book we will use the following definitions, which are also in the glossary:

Sponsor: A generic term used to describe a GP or manager in a situation where the type of entity is indeterminate.

GP: The sponsor of a transaction structured as a Limited Partnership.

Manager or Managing Member: The sponsor of a transaction structured as a Limited Liability Company.

Operator: A sponsor who also provides a full spectrum of real estate services such as property management, construction management, human resources, accounting, etc.

Normally, when securities are being sold, the SEC regulates the process to provide protections for investors, which means the company needs to comply with a variety of well-intentioned but costly regulations. Because syndicates are essentially small, standalone companies, it is cost prohibitive for them to register with the SEC as investment companies under the Investment Company Act of 1940. As a result, most real estate offerings use an exemption to the act allowing them to avoid registration; most commonly Regulation D ("Reg D"). Companies raising money through Reg D can choose to do so through multiple types of exemptions, which provide different limitations on how money can be raised. Perhaps the most common exemption used, Reg D 506(b), requires that offerings not be marketed publicly and limits the offerings to investments by "accredited investors".

An accredited investor means a wealthy and sophisticated investor or organization as defined by the SEC. Accredited means someone with a net worth of at least $1,000,000 (excluding their primary residence), or annual income of at least $200,000 individually (or $300,000 jointly with their spouse) for the past two years. (U.S. Securities & Exchange Commission 2013) 506(b) investors are allowed to self-certify that they meet accreditation requirements. In practice, this is as easy as filling out a simple form and providing it to the GP. Accredited investors are deemed to be sophisticated enough to evaluate private offerings and wealthy enough to tolerate the risk involved with investing in them. In my experience though, accreditation is a poor tool to measure appropriateness. If you aren't accredited, you can't invest in most Reg D offerings, but just because you are accredited doesn't mean you should! Even if you qualify, think carefully about the risk profile of the investment you are making and consider how it fits within your unique financial situation. Consult trusted and qualified advisers before deciding if these investments are right for you.

Because Reg D 506(b) offerings cannot be publicly marketed (for example, they aren't allowed to be posted on a company website), the distribution of offerings is usually quite limited. Interested investors need to be on a pre-defined list of potential investors, which is created by the GP through word of mouth referrals or other inefficient means. Because it is time consuming to find and register for offerings, it is difficult to compare large numbers of offerings and the quality and terms of offerings varies wildly.

If you are particularly bored, go straight to the SEC website and gorge yourself on minutiae at http://www.sec.gov/investor. Of course, there is much, much more to know about transaction structuring and legal issues. It is an insanely mind-numbing field that makes me thankful I pursued my law career no further than a practice LSAT. But this should be good enough for the moment.

We started out by discussing REITs; the standard against which other real estate products should be measured. Given the myriad benefits of REITs, why would you purposefully lock up your money for years in a syndicated deal?

In theory, and perhaps even in practice, investors require higher investment returns to compensate them for the lack of liquidity inherent in private deals. In other words, you make these investments because they have better returns than liquid alternatives like REITs. This liquidity premium is a concept that makes some intuitive sense and is referenced commonly by institutional investors but is difficult to quantify in practice. You can find plenty of academic papers on the topic if you are so inclined.

Also, syndicates are usually structured as flow-through or pass-through entities, which means items like depreciation and interest expense are passed through to individual investors. (Toder 2008) On net, this structure can be a significant tax benefit for many investors, allowing them to defer taxes to later years or offset income from other investments. An example of how this might work is below, showing the impact of these allocations on the taxable income from a $100,000 investment.

Allocated Depreciation Example

All figures based on a hypothetical $100,000 investment

Year:	1	2	3	4	5	6	7	8	9	10
Net Cash Flow /Share	5,000	5,500	6,000	6,500	7,000	7,500	8,000	8,500	9,000	9,500
Plus: Principal Reduction	0	0	2,000	2,000	2,000	2,000	2,000	2,000	2,000	2,000
Less: Expensed Capex	(1,500)	(1,500)	(750)	(750)	0	0	0	0	0	0
Less: Depreciation	(10,000)	(10,000)	(10,000)	(10,000)	(10,000)	(5,000)	(5,000)	(5,000)	(5,000)	(5,000)
Taxable Income	(6,500)	(6,000)	(2,750)	(2,250)	(1,000)	4,500	5,000	5,500	6,000	6,500
Cumulative Taxable Income	(6,500)	(12,500)	(15,250)	(17,500)	(18,500)	(14,000)	(9,000)	(3,500)	2,500	9,000

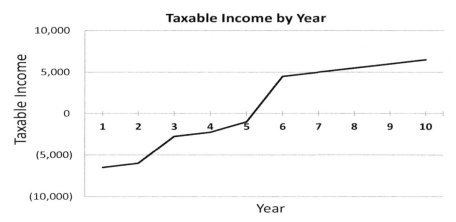

Perhaps the biggest benefit of the syndicate structure is that it allows you to evaluate the exact property that will be purchased and the syndicator's strategy for operating the real estate before you make the decision to invest. Investing in a REIT or a fund means you completely hand over the investment process to someone else. Syndicate investing means you can do your own homework on the subject property – park in the garage (are there enough spaces?), grab a sandwich at the corner deli (is there a long line for lunch?), peek in the windows (are there vacant spaces?), and drive around the neighborhood (are you scared?). You might not be running your own investment valuation models, but it's comforting to get a feel for each property and you can easily get a sense of whether you are looking at well-located and fundamentally good real estate or a poorly designed freak show of a property.

Many investors favor properties in their own city because they have such a good sense of the nuances of their neighborhoods, property uses, and traffic flows. Although skilled investors have a process for underwriting properties nearly anywhere, there is an inherent advantage to investing in your own back yard. For this reason, syndicated real estate deals are done disproportionately by local operators and funded by their local network of investors. Floods of out-of-towners out-bidding locals for properties is a notorious red flag signaling an overheated market.

One caveat: although you can evaluate the business plan in advance, most GPs retain almost total control over major decisions after the deal close; things like refinancing the property, changing the investment strategy, or selling the property. Usually LPs have some ability to override the decisions of the GP or replace the GP with another group, but it's difficult to organize and execute in practice and usually happens only when a deal is in complete meltdown. Once you buy your ticket, you're stuck on the ride whether you like it or not.

Another major benefit of private partnerships is the ability to participate in a 1031 exchange, either to defer taxes when a property is sold or to find a home for proceeds from the sale of a property you already own. Because this is an important topic, let's do a quick review of 1031s before proceeding further.

Section 1031 of the United States Internal Revenue Code allows investors to defer the recognition of capital gains when a property is sold. (U.S. Internal Revenue Service 2008) By carefully following a set of complicated rules, you can sell one property for a profit, invest the proceeds into another qualifying property, and the capital gains from your investment will be deferred until the exchange property is sold. You can continue exchanging and deferring these taxes indefinitely until you cash out or the rules are changed. Not all investment structures can take advantage of 1031s, but syndicates often can.

In a simple scenario, an exchange works as follows: First, the original property is sold. This relinquished property is known as the "downleg". The GP notifies LPs of the sale and gives them an opportunity to participate in an exchange. The sale of the downleg starts a clock; a replacement property (the "upleg") must be identified within 45 days (up to three properties can be identified), and the replacement property must be purchased within 180 days. In the meantime, investors' cash sits in a special accommodator account waiting to be re-invested. If the purchase of the replacement property requires more cash, additional equity can be raised from new investors. If it does not require all the cash sitting in the accommodator, some of the proceeds are returned to investors and a portion of the gains will be have to be recognized by investors.

In the example above, the legal structure stays essentially unchanged with a single investment entity. Alternatively, property can be purchased using exchange proceeds from multiple separate transactions, but the money cannot be combined into a single simple partnership structure. Tax law requires that the replacement property be owned in a special tenants-in-common ("TIC") structure where each exchange is an owner of the property. A simple two-TIC LLC structure could look like this:

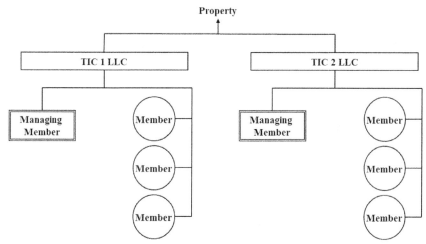

Simple Two-TIC Limited Liability Company Structure

As you can see, TIC structures can become very complex very quickly, particularly when dealing with many TICs from disparate owners. As of this writing, I'm working on a combined set of acquisitions involving four properties and twenty-four separate entities. This structure can and does work fine on a regular basis, but for reasons beyond the scope of this book it can limit the control of the GP to make major decisions or even effectively operate the property in times of distress, exacerbating a potentially bad situation. Although there are downsides to strong GP control over transactions, having a firm hand on the rudder in a storm can be helpful. Having 30 hands all pulling in different directions on the same rudder is rarely productive.

For normal syndicated deals, taking advantage of 1031 exchanges means you are stuck with the same GP. Because entity that owns the downleg and upleg can't change, investors can't switch from Joe's Office Investment Company to Dianne's Retail Investment Company and preserve their exchange benefits. Once Joe sells the office, they're stuck waiting to see what he offers his LPs as an exchange opportunity. As we discuss later, some JV investors or major investors who participate through a TIC structure may be able to work around this limitation.

There is no question that 1031s can be an important estate planning tool and that they have some legitimate benefits. Keep in mind though, that taxes are only deferred, not eliminated. They will need to be paid at some point, and without planning ahead you may trap yourself in a cycle of investing exchange dollars to avoid taxes rather than because you have good investment opportunities. If your exchange investment sours and you lose some or all of your capital, you will still owe the deferred capital gains tax. That means you may get no money out of a deal but still have a huge tax bill to pay – a dismal situation. The exchange cycle spectacularly melted down during the financial crisis when the TIC syndication boom of the mid-2000s resulted in syndicators simply closing up shop, leaving formerly passive TIC investors and foreclosing lenders to work out distressed transactions on their own. Don't let this nightmare scenario happen to you. Talk to tax and legal advisers and think carefully about the staying power of the GP and the risk of the exchange deal before participating in a TIC syndication, particularly if there are many TICs involved and the TIC entities aren't under common GP control. Deferring taxes can be a powerful tool, but investors don't usually benefit from selling properties at a market peak if they simply exchange into another deal at similarly lofty valuations.

There is at least one important exception to this comment, and it is a critical benefit of the exchange process, particularly for older investors with estate planning concerns. Under IRC § 1014(a), if the owner of a property dies and bequeaths the property, the beneficiary's basis is the market value of the property when it is bequeathed, not the basis of the original owner. This means you can actually avoid taxes, not just defer them, when you pass on property to your heirs. Taking advantage of this "stepped up basis", can significantly reduce (not just defer) taxes for investors' beneficiaries, and is a major benefit of exchanging investments to defer taxes. By definition you won't live to see the benefit, but your heirs will thank you!

Although I described the potential for exchanges as a benefit of the partnership structure, they can be either great or terrible. You may not know which adjective applies to your situation until the dust settles years from now.

I realize this section on 1031 exchanges was pretty boring, so here's a recap if you slept through it:

- Exchanges let you defer (not avoid) taxes if you sell one property and use the proceeds to buy another one.
- Exchanges are most common with syndicated deals (not funds).
- Multiple exchanges can be used to buy a property through a tenants-in-common (TIC) structure.
- Most syndicate investors can't switch between GPs and maintain their exchange.
- If you can defer taxes until you die, your heirs may really benefit.
- Don't do a bad deal just to delay taxes.
- If you're considering an exchange, consult a tax advisor because this stuff is really complicated.

Why wouldn't you want to invest in a partnership?

Unlike buying shares in publicly traded REITs, your decision to invest in a syndicated deal is a long-term commitment to the real estate and the partner. Investment periods range from two to three years on the short side (for value-add flips or development deals) to 10 to 20 years. GPs generally try to provide a liquidity event through a sale or significant refinance periodically for investors, but the market may not cooperate with their initial plans. A deal with a 10 year loan term will probably have significant prepayment penalties preventing an early sale, and if the market is in the tank when the loan comes due, the GP may decide to refinance the property and hold until the market recovers. Most organizational documents make it difficult or impossible to sell your LP interest to someone else. Even if you can sell, the secondary market for these interests is very thin, especially in times of market distress. The complicated nature of partnerships and asymmetric information between GPs and LPs means that anyone willing to buy these illiquid assets is probably going to want a significant discount to make up for the risk and trouble. Your best bet is to not put yourself in a situation where you need to sell your interests even if that means not participating in the first place. Only invest money you don't ever need to get back.

In contrast to large institutional investors, many syndicators run small, specialized operations, focused on a specific geographic and product niche, and raise money from a "friends and family" network that grows slowly by word of mouth. Being a successful syndicator self-selects a small group of people who are entrepreneurial, willing to take risks, are well connected, and are not overly concerned about the prospect of asking their friends for money. This situation has been created in part by securities laws that have until recently limited advertising investment opportunities, effectively making a rolodex of wealthy friends a prerequisite for the job.

Because of the nature of the business (which we discuss more in "Alignment of Interests"), GPs often find success by doing numerous deals rather than only quality deals. When deal flow stops, so does the fee and promote stream, making syndicators the ultimate deal junkies. Developers in particular have a well-earned reputation for doubling down repeatedly, making and losing multiple fortunes in the course of a colorful career.

These reputations don't apply across the board though, and the quality and nature of GPs varies widely. From the GP's perspective, syndication can be a stable and profitable long-term business model and many experienced and high-quality operators have carved out niches benefitting their investors and themselves.

Funds

A relative newcomer to the real estate space, comingled private equity real estate funds have grown into a dominant source of equity for the industry. The growth of leveraged buyout funds in the 1970s set the groundwork for an equivalent structure in real estate. The most influential groups in the late 1980s and early 1990s were opportunity funds formed to take advantage of the market distress during the S&L crisis and subsequent fire-sale real estate liquidations through the government-formed Resolution Trust Corporation (RTC). Sam Zell and Merrill Lynch's funds of this era were eventually taken public and ultimately became Equity Office Properties Trust, one of the most well-known REITs. (Real Property Association of Canada 2008)

Funds share some attributes with syndicates but are fundamentally different types of investments. Syndicated transactions are typically one-off opportunities allowing the investor to decide whether to invest in a specific property. The decision to invest is based on the sponsor, the property, and the business plan. In syndicated deals, you pretty much know what you're getting yourself into. In contrast, blind pool funds raise money from investors in advance based on the track record of a GP and a pre-defined strategy. Commitments are gathered into a single fund entity, and when critical mass is achieved, a "first close" occurs and the fund begins acquiring properties and drawing down capital as needed to fund the acquisitions.

Funds are mechanically similar to syndicated investments with an additional layer of ownership. Like syndicates, they are usually newly formed entities and can be either limited partnerships or limited liability companies. LPs invest in, and contribute cash into the fund entity, which is managed by the GP. Properties are purchased by the fund entity through wholly owned SPE subsidiaries, each of which is created to own a specific property. This additional layer of entities adds complexity to the structure, but protects the larger fund investment from liability caused by a single problem property and usually needs to be done regardless, since most lenders require an SPE borrower to be formed for each property. A simple org chart for a fund is shown below.

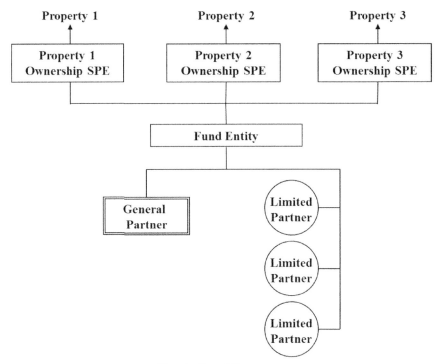

Simple Fund Structure

One of the key benefits of an investment in a fund is the diversification it can provide. While the various real estate types are still quite correlated, a variety of investments across food groups and markets should help to cut down on volatility. For single strategy funds with very similar assets (which would be expected to perform similarly and have correlated returns), the fund may not provide much diversification but may at least dilute concentration risk within the strategy. Thus, if something strange happens at a specific property – a localized environmental spill for example – other well performing deals might bring the overall fund returns back into line with what the strategy should have yielded based on the market's performance. In short, little surprises are less likely to blow up an investment. For smaller investors in particular, this helps limited investment dollars be spread over more transactions while still recognizing the other benefits of private real estate investing.

Fund investment periods may stretch over multiple years, which means equity needs to be committed before the fund can be fully invested. As a result, investors don't have the opportunity to make property-by-property investment decisions. To help alleviate this problem, some funds are "seeded" with assets in advance, showing investors a portion of the fund portfolio and at least providing some pretty photos and stories to spice up the marketing packages. GPs may purchase these investments with their own capital and contribute them to the fund (watch out for conflicts of interest based on the valuation of these assets) as part or all of their co-invest, or they may be purchased with equity from the fund's early investors.

Because investors are pooling their money to buy an unspecified group of properties, a blind pool, investors can't know in advance what their capital is buying. To help alleviate this, fund managers build in a series of limitations on funds to provide investors with comfort about how their money will be spent. Let's go through a few of the more common fund terms you should expect to see.

Fund life: Investors like to know how long their investment will remain illiquid in advance; a not unreasonable request. Private equity funds set an outside target date by which they intend to have liquidated investments and returned capital, hopefully, to investors. Usually mechanisms are in place to extend the fund life if necessary due to extreme market distress or in case a few assets haven't been able to sell for one reason or another, but most managers are loathe to use these provisions unless they absolutely have to. Some exceptions exist, such as evergreen funds or those structured as hedge-funds, but these are less common in real estate due to the difficulty and cost of regularly marking values to market. Personally I think evergreen funds are perfect for core and core-plus real estate because they allow investors to take a long-term owner's perspective and avoid unnecessary transaction costs and take advantage of 1031 exchange provisions, but… the market has spoken.

Fundraising timing: Because the fundraising process can take upwards of 12-18 months, investments often commence before the last investors commit to the deal, giving them the benefit of knowing more about the fund holdings than early investors. This information asymmetry is discussed later in the book. In short, it creates problems. To limit the problems, an outside date is set on fundraising.

Investment/re-investment period: The period of time in which new investments can be made is often limited. This helps LPs manage their own liquidity better and supports the overall investment plan. As an example, a 10-year fund may have a 3-year investment window, meaning that after the third anniversary of the first close, no new investments can be made and any remaining unfunded investor commitments will be released. In this case, if investments are expected to be longer term holds (for instance 7-10 years), it limits investments from being made so late in the fund life that they are likely to exceed the planned fund life or be forced to be liquidated earlier than the target hold date. The investment period also adds some discipline to GPs, motivating them to put investments to work, rather than to sit on idle cash for years in an effort to time the market. Obviously, this can be good or bad for investors. Some funds allow for re-investment of equity from properties sold within the re-investment window, effectively increasing the amount of investible capital in the fund.

Property limitations: Much of the value provided by GPs is their specific expertise in a niche market or product. Constraints on property type, age, and location ensure GPs stick to what they know. Or, if they don't intend to, at least you know their plans in advance. For more diversified operators or capital allocators (who invest with other operators), a mix of investments may be exactly what investors want to see. Rather than being limited to a single strategy, they may have minimum allocations to strategies, providing assurance that the fund will have some diversification across product types.

These constraints are sometimes set as "targets" (in which case the investor has no recourse if they are not adhered to, except to hold back investments from future funds), or may take effect when the fund reaches a minimum investment level (for instance, there may not be constraints until the fund is 50% invested). Obviously, the first investment in a fund will create a 100% allocation, so as a practical matter broadly diversified funds need to be materially invested before the limitations kick in.

The drawback of target allocations is an inability to take advantage of inevitable unforeseen opportunities managers run across in the normal course of business. Although real estate has become increasingly specialized, particularly in the primary "food groups" of apartments, office, retail, and industrial, there is plenty of ownership crossover among the larger more diversified players. That means portfolio sales may include multiple property types, a loan may be cross-collateralized with multiple property types, there may be an assemblage opportunity to purchase adjacent properties, or any number of other justifying situations. Interesting, unusual, and sometimes compelling opportunities pop up all the time for managers outside their area of expertise. Some simply turn them down, others are willing to stray a bit to take advantage of the remaining bits of inefficiency in an otherwise highly efficient market. Single transaction syndicators have a particularly hard time taking advantage of these situations, but funds will sometimes carve out a small segment of their allocation with a high level of flexibility to allow them to take advantage of these opportunities. In practice, minimums can be set up for each product type and geography, but the minimums may not add up to 100%, providing freedom for the GP to either go outside the stated allocation or fill the remainder with whatever deals seem most attractive within the primary strategy. This flexibility isn't necessarily bad, just make sure it's limited and defined enough to feel confident that the bulk of the fund will stay within the fund manager's area of expertise.

Deal size: To ensure enough diversification is being provided, limitations can be set on transaction sizes. For example, a fund could limit each investment to no more than 20% of the total fund size. Like other constraints, deal size limitations need to consider the fundraising timeline of the fund and provide flexibility early in the process as the GP invests toward a target allocation.

Leverage: Limits on the use of debt allow investors to evaluate how much risk can be created due to financial engineering. In practice, managing risk by limiting debt can be somewhat complicated. The most common limit is simply a target overall fund loan-to-value ratio, providing the manager with some flexibility to manage toward the target as they see fit. Because each food group, and even each individual transaction will have its own unique risk profile, not to mention the constant variations in the cost and terms of debt, it's impossible to decide in advance how much debt is appropriate. A 75% loan on a low-income apartment property with stable, strong cash flow may be more conservative than a 50% loan on a distressed vacant office building.

Real estate funds, like other investment products, may invest directly in property, invest as joint-venture equity partners with operating partners, or allocate money across other funds in a fund-of-funds format. Because costs of investments in real estate private equity are relatively high compared to other product types, the latter two strategies, and in particular the fund-of-funds strategy, can be inefficient for investors due to the combination of fees and promotes from both the fund investor and the direct investor. Although JV funds do suffer from the handicap of paying a "double promote", they add legitimate value for investors because their investments usually have the ability to control each partnership; making major decisions or even replacing the operating partner if the investment doesn't go as planned. Syndicate investments tend to have much weaker control provisions from limited partners since ownership is spread between so many parties – parties that are difficult to coordinate into action when necessary. Larger institutional JV funds are also able to negotiate much more attractive economic investment terms with operating partners, at least partially making up for the problem of double promotes.

As a side note, some funds hate to admit to investors that double promotes are charged so they create impossibly complex management agreements with incentive fee structures tied to investment outcomes. The economic result is identical to a promote, but it's called a management fee. People don't work for free as a general rule. The more people and companies are involved, the more fees need to be paid. Sometimes it makes sense to invest directly, sometimes it makes sense to partner with specialists – neither strategy is inherently bad if all groups involved are legitimately adding value to the process.

So why would someone invest in a fund rather than just investing in a series of syndications to create their own bespoke real estate portfolio? For much the same reason you might invest in a mutual fund rather than building your own stock portfolio. Picking properties and partners is time consuming and tedious if you don't happen to enjoy the process for its own sake. As mentioned previously, a single fund investment can provide better diversification for limited investment allocations, and funds have the negotiating power and size to create some efficiencies that smaller investors lack.

Finally, some investors simply value the ability to abdicate responsibility for investments to other people. As a result, funds focus on marketing a long history with many billions in experience and the imprimatur of Ivy League MBAs. Investing in funds means entrusting your money to people who, ostensibly, have devoted their careers to the art of private investing and are good at it. For those charged with putting to work other people's money (pension investors, investment advisers, etc.), fund investments are a useful way to put the responsibility of investing in the hands of other people. When the real estate market takes its next inevitable dive, they can always blame poor performance on the fund manager and switch the allocation to another manager. Plausible deniability is always a safe strategy when the pedigree of the fund is strong enough. The unfortunate reality is that careers in money management are built less on making good investments than on avoiding being fired for making investments that in retrospect look stupid.

These incentives apply to the fund management business as well. Funds tend to invest through a "herd mentality". Few funds want to be the first to jump back into riskier assets after a crash. Instead, they slowly take on increasing levels of risk, creating a coordinated momentum putting increasing money to work as the market reaches all-time highs; a self-sustaining feedback loop that continues until the next inevitable crash and retrenchment. When things go south, fund managers can take solace that their investments sucked in tandem with their very prestigious and decorated peers.

Lest I seem too cynical, I will be the first to admit that there is merit to investing with qualified and experienced experts. As we talk about repeatedly, real estate is complicated and even investing in partnerships has a surprising level of complexity. Some of the savviest investors I know work in the fund industry. But the quality varies ... widely. Don't invest in a fund because it has been sold to you. Do your own homework from the ground up to decide where you want to put your money if funds are the right vehicle for you.

Joint Venture Investments

Joint venture ("JV") investments are essentially a syndicated transaction with a single LP investor. JV investments could be made by a single private investor or through a co-mingled fund that invests with operating partners as described above. The structure of JV investments mirrors a syndicate LP or LLC structure, but without multiple investors:

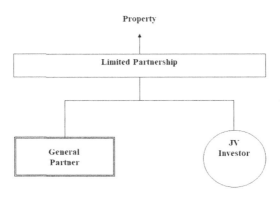

Simple JV Structure

Because the single LP typically puts in between 80% to 95% of the equity, they have much stronger control provisions in deals and are able to negotiate better terms. As an example, JV investors can usually time investment sales or exchanges, allowing them to coordinate transactions across their portfolio and avoiding forced liquidations at inopportune times by the GP or other investors.

The primary downside to JV investments for investors is the large amount of equity required for each deal. This might not be an issue for larger investors, but for the majority of private investors, typical deal sizes are out of reach or too large to allow for sufficient diversification.

From the perspective of the GP, JV transactions can simplify the acquisition process by limiting the number of investors to organize and eliminating the sales process from the deal timeline. Despite the less profitable structure, it may be worthwhile if there are no other good sources for equity and the alternative is not doing the deal.

More time is devoted specifically to the JV model later in the book.

Crowdfunded Transactions

Crowdfunding refers to the practice of raising money from a large group of people through an online portal. The popularity of crowdfunding has exploded over the past few years, led by sites like Indiegogo and Kickstarter. Because of regulations limiting the ability to advertise securities, these sites mostly raised money to back creative projects or fund the purchase of products in advance.

This is great if you want to support an indie documentary about tattoo artists or a new flashlight design, but not particularly helpful for entrepreneurs trying to seed or grow a business. With the passage of the Jumpstart Our Business Startups (JOBS) Act in 2012, securities regulations were changed, making crowdfunding real estate transactions and other equity investments possible.

As we have discussed, because of securities regulations, private real estate investments have traditionally been highly opaque and distributed either through word-of-mouth or highly inefficient broker-dealer channels. The growth of crowdfunding has the potential to be highly disruptive to the traditional model, revolutionizing the way investments are marketed and made. Even the simple fact that offerings are now available for review online makes comparing fees and investment structures easier than ever, putting pressure on LPs to standardize and become more competitive.

Because it is so new, the space is evolving very quickly. Real estate crowdfunding was projected to grow from a $1 billion industry in 2014 to more than $2.5 billion by the end of 2015 (massolution 2015). As of this writing, crowdfunding is operational but impractical as a standalone equity raising solution for most established LPs. An LP raising equity through a crowdfunding portal can only expect to raise $2,000,000 or so for a typical equity deal – too small for many commercial real estate transactions. As a result, crowdfunding is being incorporated as an "add on" to traditional equity raises and is being done in many cases as an experiment by LPs to understand the new technology and begin to incorporate it in their long term business strategy.

Let's start by summarizing the mechanics of crowdfunding before we get into the practical aspects of joining the crowd.

Exemptions: You will recall that private real estate investors generally need to use an exemption from securities law to avoid potentially costly compliance requirements. Crowdfunding sites use different exemptions for their offerings, depending on the deal and their investor base. These are the exemptions I see discussed most often (Moloney 2015):

- Reg D 506(b): Accredited investors only, no advertising allowed. Investors can self-certify their accreditation status. This is the same exemption typically used by private syndicators.

- Reg D 506(c): Like the 506(b) exemption but it allows offerings to be advertised. Investors need to go through a more rigorous certification process to show that they are accredited, either providing copies of financial or tax statements or have a qualified third party (like their CPA or attorney) provide a letter certifying their status.
- Reg A+ Tier 1: Advertising is allowed; investors are not required to be accredited.
- Reg A+ Tier 2: Advertising is allowed; investors are not required to be accredited, but investments are limited to 10% of income or net worth.

Both Reg A+ exemptions require SEC review, which is time consuming. This makes them more likely to be used for funds than individual property syndications. In fact, many of the crowdfunded transactions I have reviewed appear to be standard 506(c) or 506(b) offerings made to a list of accredited investors, but with the benefit of slick websites that make the review of investment documents and tracking investment returns easier for investors. Because crowdfunding is so new in the real estate industry, sponsors and capital raising groups are still in the process of experimenting to find the best way to incorporate them into their businesses.

Structure: If you are considering a crowdfunded investment, pay attention to the investment structure and the fees involved. Different crowdfunding platforms are making use of different structuring strategies, each of which has benefits and drawbacks. The simplest structure is essentially identical to the traditional syndicate model. Crowdfunding investors participate directly in the offering as LPs, subscribing for interests directly with the GP.

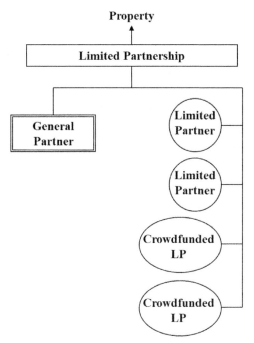

Direct Crowdfunding Structure

Alternatively, the crowdfunding company can set up an SPE into which people can invest. That SPE then invests as an LP in a partnership and passes through cash flows and investment reporting information to the crowd. This potentially simplifies the reporting and investor relations process for the GP, although this is only true to the extent that the GP doesn't already have many other individual LPs to service (a rare situation). Another feature of this arrangement is that it allows the crowdfunding platform to easily charge an additional layer of fees and/or promote to their investors, adding to the overall load in the transaction. This replicates the double promote structure discussed earlier in the allocator fund model.

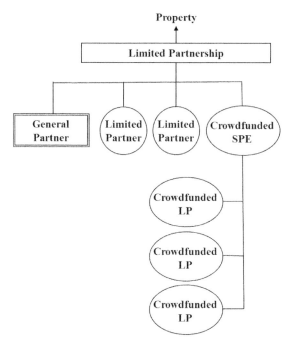

Intermediate Crowdfunding Structure

In either case, crowdfunding has the potential to significantly increase the number of investors in each offering and bring many new investors to the table. This creates new risks for both GPs and LPs and an additional layer of investor relations support needed to service the larger number of LPs.

Fees: Crowdfunding companies need to make money, which means they need to charge fees. Because the space is so new and quickly changing, the amounts and types of fees still vary and there are a few different business models being implemented by the various players. The most common fees are:

- Charging GPs a set fee to administer the offering
- Charging GPs fundraising fees, typically a percentage of the equity raised
- Charging LPs administrative or asset management fees for administering the offering
- Charging LPs an additional level of promote (double promote) in addition to the promote charged by the GP

These fees aren't mutually exclusive, and different crowdfunding companies charge different combinations and amounts. Each company claims vehemently that their structure is the best, which leads to some entertaining industry conference sessions. In reality, crowdfunding platforms need to provide access to quality investments to attract investors, need to have a large rolodex of investors and money-raising capability to attract quality GPs, and need to charge sufficient fees to be profitable. Time will tell what structures fare best in this competitive marketplace, and in the meantime it will be interesting to watch the process unfold.

Crowdfunding is important for the industry because it has the potential to introduce a new set of investors to private real estate and because it provides a competitive platform where accredited investors can evaluate many offerings from many GPs and sample them in smaller investment increments. This increased visibility and transparency will put pressure on industry players to become more competitive and standardized in their offerings. It will also increase the importance of the marketing function at investment companies, which is a new skill since it hasn't been allowed until recently for most private real estate offerings.

Because real estate crowdfunding is so new, it has some wild-west aspects, which are evident in many of the deals raising money on the sites. This has as much or more to do with the demand profile of investors on these sites as it does with the sponsors or crowdfunding sites preferences. At a National Multifamily Housing Counsel event in September 2015, Doug Miller, the cofounder and CEO of Fundrise said, "We definitely are surprised by what the crowd wants. We started with [conservative] deals where investors weren't going to lose money. But the investors often want high risk... They also want short term. They'd rather take a nine-month deal rather than a nine-year deal." (Haughey 2015) My unofficial review of offerings on multiple crowdfunding sites, has uncovered a wide disparity in offerings in terms of sponsor quality, terms for LPs, control provisions, and overall deal quality. A number of the offerings I reviewed have extremely high fees to LPs, obvious conflicts of interests, material fees paid to related entities, non-market promote structures and other generally egregious terms. In fairness to the crowdfunding sites, GPs generally set the terms of their own offerings rather than conform to standard offering terms imposed by a crowdfunding platform. These fundraising sites are intermediaries, connecting predominantly risk-seeking investors with generally aggressive sponsors. The crowd has spoken, at least for the moment.

When the market takes its next turn for the worse, there is a real possibility that investors will be hurt and the crowdfunding and real estate industry will develop a bad reputation. I hope this isn't the case. The crowdfunding movement has the potential to be a powerful force for good (or at least for efficiency). Over time, increased transparency has the potential to improve the overall quality of offerings and create more uniformity of terms. Hopefully, these market forces will improve the quality of offerings naturally and the industry will avoid backlash when the next inevitable downturn happens.

Secondary Investments

A primary transaction in private real estate is an LP investing in a deal or a fund through a normal offering process arranged by a GP. The secondary market refers to the practice of LPs buying and selling LP interests from each other after the initial fundraising process has concluded.

Secondary transactions could happen for several reasons. Often secondary sales are motivated by the need to rebalance an overall investment portfolio. For instance, if an LP starts with a 20% allocation to private real estate and the value of other investments deviates significantly from the value of the real estate allocation, they will need to rebalance by adding or subtracting from their real estate holdings to maintain their target allocation. Sometimes unexpected events could create an immediate need for cash, so an investor could be motivated to sell a private investment before it is liquidated by the GP. Because real estate transactions can last up to 10 years or longer, this is not particularly unusual. 10 years is a long time… things happen.

Regardless of the reason, sellers of secondary interests usually have to accept a discounted price for their investment. Many GPs place restrictions on secondary sales of interests, often requiring GP approval before an investment can be sold to another LP. Also, while there is a sub-specialty of investors who focus on purchasing secondary interests, the secondary market for private real estate is relatively small in comparison to the primary market (PEI/PERE 2012). There is no central market for most secondary transactions so finding a qualified buyer of LP interests is not necessarily a simple process. In short, if you are investing in private real estate, you should not count on being able to sell your investment on the secondary market before it is liquidated by the GP. If you want to get out early, you may either be forced to take a significant haircut or be prohibited entirely.

CHAPTER 2: EVALUATING DEALS - PRODUCTS, STRATEGIES, & CAPITAL STRUCTURES

"Unlike a well-defined, precise game like Russian roulette, where the risks are visible to anyone capable of multiplying and dividing by six, one does not observe the barrel of reality." – Fooled by Randomness – Nassim Nicholas Taleb

Learning to comprehensively evaluate the infinite variations of commercial property deals is a career-long endeavor for many professionals, and certainly more than we can cover in a single chapter. Nevertheless, even investors who entrust the detailed work to GPs need to have enough background to decide how they want to allocate their investments across various product types and to understand common risks. Understanding these basic issues will improve your ability to evaluate investment opportunities, helping you ask better questions and make better decisions. Most books on real estate spend 90% of their time on this topic, but we will spend significantly less, just touching on major issues and considerations to help you understand and effectively review potential offerings.

Product Types

The term "Product Type", also known in industry parlance as "Food Group" often describes how a property is used (although it can also sometimes refer to the type of investment structure). The major categories of food groups are office, retail, industrial, and multifamily. Each major category has sub-specialties, such as medical office, strip retail, big-box retail, regional malls, flex industrial, distribution, affordable housing, and senior housing. Other product types don't fit cleanly within these categories and are considered specialty asset classes like golf courses or marinas.

Each product type has unique issues to consider and requires expertise, so owner/operators tend to specialize in one (sometimes more) product type, requiring investors to either partner with multiple operators or invest in a fund who handles this allocation on their behalf. Rare is the hands-on experienced operator who has true expertise and necessary industry relationships across a wide range of product types. Even many extremely large investors, such as REITs stay within the confines of a single product or sub-product type.

Let's discuss very briefly the major product types you're likely to run across:

Office

Office - where people go to sit at their desk, talk on the phone, and click their mouse. Office buildings used to be easier to re-purpose for different types of tenant uses but have become increasingly specialized over time. Because of the unique needs of each tenant, large costs are incurred to customize space when a new tenant moves in. These costs, known across commercial property types as "Tenant Improvements" or "TIs", can be moderate for simple changes such as flooring, lighting, and paint, but can grow exponentially for specialty uses that require costly upgrades to building services such as heating, ventilation, and air-conditioning ("HVAC") systems. Landlords often split these costs with tenants depending on market strength, the uniqueness of the tenant needs, and what they can negotiate.

Landlords also commonly need to pay a commission to leasing brokers ("Leasing Commissions", or "LCs") who find tenants for their vacant space. LCs vary but are commonly in the range of 5% of the total rent during the term of a lease. Collectively, TIs and LCs can be a major cash expense for landlords and tend to be most material for office deals. Furthermore, these expenses can hit a deal exactly when a property has significant vacancy and may not have enough cash flow to cover them, so it is critical that operators plan ahead, putting money aside in a reserve account for potential expenses before they are actually needed. Many lenders require these reserves, some do not. Depending on how many tenants are in a particular building, and the uniformity of timing of the lease expirations, cash flow can be volatile with office deals as cash is reserved, and returned or spent depending on the outcome of tenant negotiations.

Office leases are generally medium-long term leases (3-5 or more years), which means that quick increases in market rents may not be translated immediately into cash flow improvements from the investment. The lost income from leases at below-market rates is known as "loss to lease". In rising markets, a big loss to lease combined with a concentration of lease expirations could be an opportunity for a landlord to renegotiate leases with existing tenants and improve operations, but these situations can be risky if many tenants move out, triggering large TI/LC expenses. In quickly declining markets, properties can benefit from the opposite situation; "gain to lease", where leases are locked in at above-market rates. Although many leases have personal or corporate guarantees, investors should expect some leases to be renegotiated by distressed tenants who are simply unable to pay their rents, so revenue may decline even without lease rollovers.

Older office buildings have increasingly become functionally obsolete (a concept discussed more later) as corporate office space planning has changed. Companies have been trending toward more collaborative workspace with smaller isolated space set aside for each employee. This means the number of employees in each square foot of office space has gone up over time. While it's easy to buy smaller cubicles and knock down some walls, higher density uses also put strains on HVAC systems, bathroom facilities, and parking ratios. It's important to keep in mind the suitability of a particular building for the types of companies in the area who are likely to be growing in the near future.

Retail

Retail – where people go to buy things and eat. The most common types of retail properties are regional malls (destination shopping experiences, often with one or more large stores acting as "anchor tenants" that draw people in to the mall), big-box (with a single large tenant), strip retail (small shops clustered together, often in a strip along a road), and anchored/grocery anchored (a combination of a large tenant, often a grocery store, and many remora-like smaller tenants providing other synergistic services).

Retail properties, like office properties, tend to have longer-term leases and require TI/LC expenses to repurpose space for new tenants. Although it varies by use, TIs for retail are often lower than office on a per square foot basis. While location is important for all properties, it is especially critical for retail buildings, particularly those whose tenants rely on drive-by traffic to bring in customers. Buildings need to be well suited for their location, capable of accommodating the right mix of tenants to attract local demand.

The combination of tenants in a retail center is synergistic (much more so than most office), which means losing a single important tenant could hurt the prospects for all tenants in a property and have a disproportionate impact of the viability of the center as a whole. In downturns, it may make sense for tenants to vacate their space before their lease term has expired. These "dark" tenants may continue to pay rent, but they no longer draw people into the center, hurting all the tenants in the property. Retail is one of the few situations in real estate where rent can be set based on the success of the tenant. Many retail leases include "percentage rent" clauses whereby a portion of sales above a certain threshold amount are split with the landlord. Thus, the property owner is incentivized to see to it that the property overall is successful and pick tenants accordingly.

Retail has steadily been impacted by changing shopping trends as people increasingly buy certain types of products online, or at least comparison shop there. Shoppers also have gravitated more lately to outdoor open-air shopping centers rather than older indoor regional malls. All products need to deal with changes in demand, but it seems that retail has really borne the brunt of changes in taste and economic trends over the past few years. The gap between good retail and bad retail properties is increasingly large and becoming more expensive to bridge.

Industrial

Industrial – where people go to make and distribute things. For some industrial users, properties are as simple as a box to keep the wind and rain out while they can get on with their business. Increasingly though, industrial properties need to technically keep up with the needs of their tenants by providing enough power, HVAC, and clear height (interior ceiling height) to accommodate each user's specific needs. Not merely a matter of preference, these technical details can be a deal-breaker for tenants who are unlikely to change their business processes to save a few cents per foot on rent in an outdated building. Flex space describes a building with an office and an industrial component, providing a single location for companies to house multiple functions of their business.

Like office and retail, industrial properties have medium to long term leases and require infusions of TI/LC capital when tenants change. TI costs tend to be relatively low for industrial properties unless a major system upgrade is required, and many industrial properties trade at much lower per square foot metrics than their office or retail counterparts.

Picking the right industrial property requires a thorough understanding of building systems and likely tenant requirements. In addition, location can be critical for some industrial users, particularly tenants doing distribution who may need to be located on specific freeway corridors or near major ports or airports.

Multifamily

Multifamily – people's homes. Once considered an outcast among commercial real estate product types, multifamily has earned a place with investors and become a mainstream institutionally owned product type.

Multifamily generally refers to apartment buildings offered for rent over short-medium terms (usually 12 months, although shorter and longer lease terms are usually available). These relatively shorter lease terms mean that revenues tend to respond faster to market movements (up or down) than other commercial property types. Because leases are constantly rolling in larger properties, managers of high-quality properties who stay on top of property operations can usually keep buildings stabilized above 90% in normal market conditions by fine-tuning rental rates. Increasingly, software systems such as LRO or Yieldstar are used to pick rents dynamically in the same way that airlines constantly change ticket prices. This ability to maintain occupancy means properly managed, solid-quality, well-located multifamily properties tend to have less revenue volatility than other commercial property types.

The quality of a multifamily property is a little more intuitive than other property types; it's the type of place you would want to live. Modern and well-maintained buildings near local amenities and freeways that have high quality unit interiors are the best. These properties command a premium in rents and handle downturns better than others.

Multifamily has a few common sub-categories. Mixed-use multifamily properties usually have a retail component at street level with units on upper floors. Mixed use is encouraged by cities who like the idea of promoting walkable neighborhoods, but many recently developed properties have struggled to lease their retail space. These spaces are often not suitable for major national tenants due to their location or size, so they can be tough to keep leased at attractive rates. Also, many multifamily groups don't have enough retail space to have the negotiating power, market knowledge, and expertise to operate retail efficiently so it's often underutilized.

Student housing is specialty apartment product built near schools and tailored specifically to the needs of students. Many student deals are rented on a "by the bed" basis, where each resident pays for a bedroom and shares a living room and kitchen with roommates. Location and walkability are particularly important with student deals, and many of these properties compete by offering extravagant gyms, pools, study areas, and other amenities. Student deals can be complicated to run, with a short leasing window available at the end of summer break, and operational issues that are unique to having a building full of younger residents.

Properties with regulatory agreements are common. "Reg agreements" come in different forms, such as income restrictions (residents' incomes must be below a certain level, often in relationship to household incomes in the area), age restrictions (residents must be over a certain age), or rent restricted (rents must stay below a certain level, often linked to area incomes) and may apply to some or all of the units in a property. LIHTC (pronounced "lie-tech") investments are another sub-category of investments that have special tax benefits for some investors and create significant restrictions on operations and compliance requirements.

Other/Specialty Products

Properties that don't fall cleanly into these categories are of course still an important fabric in the real estate tapestry. Self-storage (increasingly institutional but still a highly fragmented industry), hotels, assisted living, server farms, marinas, golf courses, RV parks, and other less common properties are all standard offerings. The fact that they fall outside the purview of the major food groups can be both a blessing and a curse. Each strategy requires its own unique skill set and relationships to be successfully executed, and the less liquid market for these properties means that they can be tougher to sell in good times or bad. On the other hand, experienced operators can take advantage of these less liquid markets and other's lack of experience to earn better risk-adjusted returns than might be available through the normal institutional product types. If you choose to invest in these properties, make sure you spread your investments among a few different strategies and pick operators with extensive experience operating similar properties.

NNN (Triple Net)

Triple net leased ("NNN") properties refer to properties leased by generally high-quality tenants for long periods of time. These leases are structured such that tenants pay for taxes, insurance, and all building maintenance. Because the tenants shoulder these risks and handle the associated issues, these investments are often low-risk and steady, if modest, income generators for investors.

Land Investments

While land is an ingredient in each of the major food groups, investing in land is a highly specialized subset of real estate investing. Land banking generally just refers to buying and holding land, while land entitlement involves pursuing entitlements from a local authority to add value before selling to a developer. Because land investments don't generate operating cash flows like their commercial real estate brethren, they require different time horizons and capital structures then other real estate investments. Also, the benefit of allocated depreciation to partners largely doesn't apply for unimproved land deals.

We will mostly avoid land banking for the purposes of this book with a few exceptions. To understand why land is so different requires some intuition about how land is valued. Later, we will discuss the valuation process in more detail, but in summary, land value is the residual value when you subtract the costs of developing a property from its ultimate stabilized value. Because property values and construction costs can be volatile, the underlying land values can be wildly erratic. Since land is very valuable when property values are high, and nearly worthless when property values are lower than construction costs, it's helpful to think about land deals as investments in call options on the real estate market rather than investments in cash flowing assets. Indeed, many of the financial world's tools used to value options on securities can also be applied to land investments.

Like all product types, land investments require very experienced and well-connected operators to successfully execute. Unlike other product types, they can require extremely long hold periods and can be highly risky depending on how the investments are structured. Keep this different risk/return profile in mind if you are considering allocating capital to land investments.

Evaluating a Property

Unless you are investing in a blind-pool fund, it's not enough to simply pick a manager and a product type. If you invest in syndicated transactions, you will at some point need to pick a specific property or properties to invest in. While some of the topics discussed in this book are nuanced and complex, identifying plain old good real estate is usually pretty simple; something non-experts can do. If a property is in a good neighborhood with good economic prospects, is easy to get to with plenty of parking, and seems attractive and generally the kind of place you wouldn't mind spending time, it's probably good real estate. If, on the other hand, it's surrounded by easily developed dirt or a blighted neighborhood and looks like hasn't been updated since the Kennedy administration, it's probably junk.

There is a school of thought that any deal is a good deal at the right price. There may or may not be some truth to that, but my general experience is that the world has plenty of investors who are willing to overpay for bad real estate, mostly with the strategy of doing some superficial work and selling it to the next sucker. That market dries up quickly at the first sign of a hiccup in real estate fundamentals. My personal opinion is that long-term investors are better served by avoiding junk without a truly exceptional reason. Let's go through the key issues to consider as you evaluate property to decide if it's something you want to invest in.

Tangible Stuff: Sticks & Bricks

Evaluating the physical attributes of a property is one of the key areas where a strong manager can earn their keep; the array of building designs and construction materials makes a comprehensive review of this topic in a single book (let alone a few paragraphs) effectively impossible. In addition to ordering and evaluating third party reports, discussed more below, managers should have the experience and knowledge of their specific asset class to be able to thoroughly evaluate properties on their own and identify any shortcomings or potential issues that may crop up in the foreseeable future.

Even though you will likely be relying on a manager for this advice, knowing a few basics is helpful so you can better understand offering materials and ask the right questions about potential investments. In this section, we will describe some of the major systems and discuss the potential impact they might have on an investment.

Comprehensive offering documents provided by the deal syndicator will provide a wealth of information about the property itself, including all the obvious things: year built, type of construction, property size and number of buildings, common area amenities, major mechanical systems and construction types, and site/floor plans. Diligent GPs will be doing their own thorough due diligence on the property and will have verified this information. At the least, they will order third party reports (aka "Thirds") to identify potential problems. The most common thirds are:

- Survey: A map of the property, showing a variety of information, such as property lines, building locations, improvements such as landscaping and parking, access, utilities, easements, and other important information.
- Physical Needs Assessment (PNA)/Property Condition Assessment (PCA or PCNA): A description of all major systems and a summary of the construction and condition of each. Roofs, plumbing, electrical, HVAC, fire, and others will all be covered. Perhaps most helpfully, a schedule is provided showing the anticipated life of each system and cost to replace it – essentially a capital roadmap for expected spending during the anticipated hold period.
- Environmental: The two most common types of environmental reports are Phase I and Phase II reports. Phase I reports search through the history

of the subject property and adjacent properties to identify potential hazards. Assuming the property wasn't previously a gas station littered with old underground storage tanks and it's in a suburban area with no problematic neighbors, the report will probably come back clean. In more urban areas with many prior uses on each site or mixed-use neighborhoods, it is hard for engineers to determine remotely how clean the property is. In these cases, the engineer will recommend a phase II report, which usually involves actually going to the site and taking samples of the soil at various locations and depths. The samples are sent to a lab to test for problematic chemicals. Environmental issues have the potential to be catastrophic for investors. The cost to fix even small issues can quickly spiral out of control. Because of the complexities involved, some GPs totally avoid properties with environmental problems while a few specialize in remediation. If there are any environmental issues at all on a deal under review, make absolutely sure the GP is qualified and experienced enough to deal with them.

• Seismic: An engineering report designed to forecast the amount of damage likely to be caused by large earthquakes. By reviewing the type of construction, materials, and location of the property, engineers estimate the percentage of loss that would be likely to occur under various earthquake scenarios. If forecast damage is too high, lenders will require extremely expensive earthquake insurance coverage for the property (impacting value by decreasing operating income), or require earthquake retrofit work to be performed to make up for poor or obsolete construction techniques and materials.

• Appraisal: A supposedly arms-length valuation of the property, which will be discussed more in our chapter on valuations and modeling.

If you're feeling curious or have some time to kill, it's not unreasonable to ask for copies of third-party reports from the GP. If you have specific questions about the property, these reports are the quickest place to go for answers. Unfortunately, while they are always comprehensive, they are not necessarily accurate. While some buyers order thirds for their own use, they are more typically ordered by the lender as part of their due diligence review before providing a loan commitment. With reports papering the file, lenders can sleep well at night knowing that if (when?) the property comes back to them with major physical issues it won't be their fault; it will be the engineer's. Lenders are concerned about making loans and not losing their job – they are not all investing their own money and don't always take an owner's approach to reviewing real estate.

This dynamic creates some poor incentives for report providers. If reports come back showing problems, deals blow up. Lenders like making loans and owners like buying property. Neither is generally happy when a diligent engineer delivers a conservative report that kills their deal. Thus, reports tend to underestimate the severity of problems and the likely cost of ownership. In fact, engineers will provide debt reports (in accordance with industry standards but usually showing fewer issues) or equity reports (which are usually more conservative) depending on what the client requests (Grossman 2013). So, while you can count on basic information about the property being correct, I would take with a very large grain of salt the conclusions drawn by many reports.

Because of this problem, diligent owners looking for quality information about properties in due diligence either contract equity reports or perform their own due diligence with their own staff or trusted engineers. Thorough physical due diligence usually requires bringing roofers, plumbers, electricians, landscapers, and other contractors out to the property to review major systems and provide quotes upfront for work that will need to be done.

Mechanical systems and structural systems are also important to review, to understand if any of the major systems are failing and if so, plans for addressing the issue. For longer term holds, you also need to know if systems will last through the planned investment period. History may not be a good guide here, particularly with newer properties being sold just as systems are starting to show their age. Even older properties may have uneven capital needs due to the timing of previous renovations. Major systems such as roofs, siding, HVAC, or plumbing, could be extremely expensive to fix but occur only occasionally. A plan needs to be in place to handle potential issues and you should understand if capital is being set aside upfront (perhaps inefficient from an IRR standpoint), or taken from operating cash flow (could impact cash distributions or create a cash shortage) to pay for the repairs.

Location

A property's location is what sets it apart from other competitors, the attribute that can never be replicated by other properties. It's true that location is critical to a property's success, but the importance of that factor depends quite a bit of the type of property and the target tenant profile. While important, location is generally not the most complicated factor to consider when evaluating properties. I try to break it into two separate considerations: macro and micro location.

Macro, as the name suggests, considers the overall quality of the metropolitan area and market within the metro area. This is often more of a hurdle issue than a quantitative valuation issue. Primary markets (New York, San Francisco, Chicago, Los Angeles, etc.) are widely considered by institutional investors to be the best places to invest. Secondary markets could refer to less desirable locations surrounding primary markets, or to smaller cities like Portland, Salt Lake City, Austin, and the like. Tertiary markets are areas one further step removed. Like building qualities ("A", "B", or "C"), locations tend to be overstated, so it's rare to hear of an owner/operator boasting about their tertiary market investment strategy no matter how many tumbleweeds are blowing across the parking lot.

Micro, as you have no doubt guessed by now, refers to the specific location and layout of a property within a submarket. Micro location considers things like proximity to nearby amenities (grocery stores, freeways, shopping malls), access to public transportation, drive-by visibility, ingress/egress (a fancy way of talking about how you get on and off a property) from nearby streets, school quality, traffic counts, crime rates, and local demographic trends.

Positioning in the Marketplace

Like locations, buildings' physical characteristics (design, functionality, materials, and state of repair) are generally classified in one of three classes of quality: A, B, or C, with C being the lowest. Class and location are sometimes referred to in combination, such as "a B in an A location". When thinking about the overall desirability of a property, it's important to think about a property in the context of the other properties it competes with. B properties in a neighborhood that is generally C may perform differently during a downturn than the same B properties in an otherwise A neighborhood.

As properties get older, they inevitably decline in quality unless significant money is invested in them to maintain their competitive place in the market. Relative positioning stays relatively constant unless new money is re-invested in properties through value-add renovations. New developments can really throw off the quality mix in a market though. Most of the time, new developments are the best designed, highest quality properties in a market. It's rare that it makes economic sense for developers to create B properties, although it can occasionally happen. More often, the delivery of shiny new properties makes the rest of the market seem a bit dated in comparison. Over time, the new developments fill up the category of A product and the formerly A properties become the new B properties.

Erosion of Relative Quality Over Time

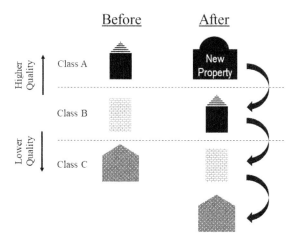

As a property gets older and becomes more functionally obsolete, the most economical course of action for an investor may be to let it drop down the quality spectrum. Having the best quality building is not always the best investment. Money is just as green coming out of ugly buildings as pretty ones.

Tenants & Investment Strategy

Let's set aside for a moment the physical attributes of a property and talk about the people part. For a property to be a solid long-term performer, it can't be functionally obsolete. In other words, is it lacking attributes that make it attractive, efficient, and useable for your target tenants? To know this, we have to know something about both the building, its competitors, and our target tenants. For example:

- Older apartment buildings built before washer/dryers were common; for gentrifying generation-X families, walking to a laundromat may be a non-starter.
- Office buildings designed for large corporations but now serving smaller tech companies; higher density (employees per square foot) users stretch the capacity of the original design, making parking and restrooms in short supply and overwhelming HVAC systems and elevators.
- Enclosed malls; the older "X" shaped multi-anchor mall is as out of fashion as '80s neon spandex. Wait, that's fashionable again? Ignore that analogy. Old malls are being beat by newer outdoor centers. If you're investing in older retail, you either need a creative business plan or you're betting on trends to move back your way.

move back your way.

These are just a few examples to demonstrate the issue. Just to be clear, there is a lot of obsolete real estate in the world, especially in urban centers. I'm not recommending to completely avoid functionally obsolete real estate, just to understand what you're getting into.

Once the property fit with tenants is understood, it's time to evaluate the specific leasing strategy for the property. Most commercial properties have a small enough list of tenants that each lease and each tenant need to be carefully reviewed. Tenant improvements and leasing commissions are so costly for office, retail, and some industrial spaces that the unexpected loss of a good tenant can be at best inconvenient and at worst catastrophic. Careful investors review all the information they can get about each tenant (financial or sales information is sometimes provided) to estimate the risk that they will leave when the lease term expires or default and go dark even earlier.

Beyond underwriting each tenant, it's important to think about lease concentration risk. In other words, do all your leases expire around the same time? If so, the property could be in the unfortunate situation of having limited (or no) cash flow while needing to pay big expenses to re-lease space. Find out if reserves are being set aside from cash flow to handle TI/LC expenses upon rollover. This is sometimes required by lenders depending on the lease rollover schedule, but not always.

If leases are significantly below market rates, losing tenants could be a good thing. This built-in "loss to lease", or the amount of lost revenue associated with below-market rate leases, can be an opportunity to increase NOI (the income available after all operating expenses and recurring capital, but before one-time capital or extraordinary events) and add value to a property with minimal investment. Just keep in mind that market conditions can change quickly. Today's loss to lease can quickly become next month's gain to lease, switching those short-term leases into an impending calamity.

Products like apartments and self-storage have more tenants and shorter lease terms, making underwriting each lease impractical, or at least less useful. While diligent operators will audit leases and review available information for these properties, more time is spent focusing on the current and future state of the market and examining comparable rental properties to determine current market rates for leases as they expire. Many apartment properties have upwards of 60% to 70% annual turnover, which means these properties feel the impact of market movements (up or down) much faster than other commercial product types.

Regardless of the property type, a market study of comparable properties (proximate and of similar vintage) is important to determine if the subject property leases are above, at, or below market rates. For some properties, the leasing strategy is simple: 1) Identify market rates, 2) Wait for leases to re-set to market, 3) Sit back and collect checks.

Other times, more heavy lifting is involved. For value-add properties, the operator is either improving the properties physically or operationally to make them more attractive to tenants and to generate more revenue. It's possible to create market data to support physical improvements by comparing your property as you envision it upon completion of the renovation to the "upside comps" in the market study. When all the work is done, do the rents seem reasonable for the finished product in comparison to other comps? There is at least as much art as science to this process and changes in market trends can quickly change the value of improvements for better or worse. Adding value through improved operations, while it's a legitimate strategy, is harder to build a business case for. Great customer service is nearly always valued by tenants but how much are they willing to pay for it? The answer to that question varies greatly by market, tenant profile, and based on tenants' other options.

The Capital Stack

Investing in real estate is capital intensive. In other words, it takes a lot of money. That money could come entirely from an equity investment, it could come from a bank providing a loan, or from some other source. Like it or not, the real estate industry is full of financial structuring of various types and complexities. There's no way to escape it. If the world took Polonius' advice to "Neither a borrower nor a lender be", most of the industry would be collecting unemployment.

The capital stack refers to the combination of all the sources of cash needed to buy a property. Think of the capital stack as a cow being sliced into various cuts of beef. Each cut has its own unique features and is used for different things. Different people enjoy different cuts – some like marbled ribeyes, some like hamburgers. In the same way, the capital stack (the types of investments making up ownership in real estate) is sliced into various products. Different investors want to buy different parts, from lenders who look for a safe bond-like investment to equity investors who look for growth and upside. Some structure is a normal and healthy way to capitalize real estate, but overly complicated structuring (referred to derisively as financial engineering) can create an accident waiting to happen.

The graphic below shows some common variations on transaction capitalizations. Investments toward the bottom of the stack are safer but have less upside, and those toward the top are more risky but have more potential for outsized investment returns. Although there are endless variations, the following products are common and worth describing in some detail:

A) All-cash / all-equity

B) Debt & equity
C) Senior debt, subordinate debt & equity
D) Senior debt, preferred equity, & common equity

Common Capitalization Structures

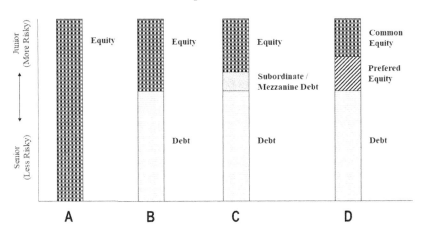

A) All Cash / All Equity

Buying a property entirely with cash/equity is the simplest and most conservative of all capitalization structures. Without required payments to a lender, it is much harder (but not impossible!) to default and get into trouble. All cash investments are commonly used for highly risky or highly illiquid investments, like land entitlement deals, that don't produce regular cash flows.

Although truly all cash transactions are somewhat rare in the commercial real estate world, they are commonly modeled as a reference point for investment returns. By modeling transactions as all cash and with the proposed capital structure, investors can consider how the financial structuring is changing investment returns. In these situations, all-cash returns are commonly referred to as "unlevered" returns. Because unlevered returns strip out the effects of financial engineering, many investors set minimum unlevered return thresholds for their investments as a way to focus on fundamentally good real estate investments rather than deals with high returns manufactured through complicated financial engineering.

B) Debt

Using a combination of debt and equity is the most common way to capitalize real estate. In this case, a lender makes a loan to the owner of the property. That loan is usually secured by the real estate, which means if the loan defaults, the lender can foreclose and become the proud new owner of the property. The loan amount is limited by the lender's risk tolerance, and is often constrained by loan to value, debt coverage ratio, debt yield, or other metrics discussed later. Various lenders are willing to take different amounts of risk and are comfortable with different product types so there can be a fair amount of variation between quotes on the same property. Commercial mortgage brokers make a living by guiding their borrower clients through this process and obtaining the most attractive financing for a given project.

The lender doesn't participate in the profits if the property does well; they simply get a return on their money for the term of the loan, then get their money back at expiration if all goes well. As a result, they try to minimize potential risk and charge a higher rate for taking on higher amounts of risk. There are two broad categories of risk, described generally in the graphic that follows:

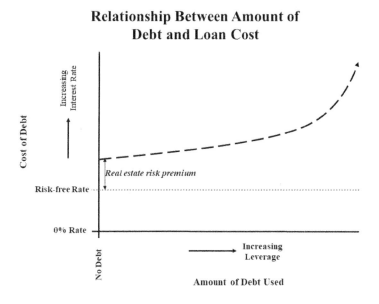

Relationship Between Amount of Debt and Loan Cost

The first is labeled the real estate risk premium. This is the unavoidable risk of being involved in a real estate company. The borrower could commit fraud, a tenant could slip, fall, and sue, the borrower could declare bankruptcy, the property could have an uninsured loss due to mold claims, etc. Stuff happens. These risks exist even in low leverage deals so lenders want to be paid a premium over what they would receive from a relatively risk-free alternative such as a bond from the United States government (about as safe a bet as there is in this world).

The second type of risk is related directly to the loan and its terms. Making payments to the lender decreases the cash flow available, increasing the chance that cash flow won't be sufficient to cover operating expenses, necessary capital expenses, and the lender's payments. (The lender is mostly indifferent to paying expected distributions to equity investors as long as they get their money!) Upon a capital event like a sale or refinance, there is risk that the proceeds won't be enough to repay the lender in full. These risks increase as the loan size increases, so lenders charge higher rates as the loan size increases to compensate for the added risk. Of course, a higher rate itself creates additional risk by further stressing operating cash flow, a factor that is considered by the lender in the course of their underwriting and pricing process. "Hard money" lenders in particular specialize in making risky loans to borrowers at high interest rates and being more than happy to foreclose and take over properties. At the high-risk end of the spectrum are "loan to own" shops that specialize in desperate borrowers and actively root for them to default.

An incredible array of loan products exists to finance real estate, and picking the right type of loan is much more than finding the lender with the lowest rate. The amount, cost, and terms of the loan need to be matched correctly with the business plan for the property. Loans that aren't well suited for an investment could at best limit flexibility and decrease investment returns, and at worst trigger a default and cause investors to lose money. While there are many sub-categories, the following descriptions are most commonly used to categorize loans. Loans in each of these categories usually share common structures and terms, which are described in more detail later in the book.

Land Loans: As the name suggests, these are loans placed on land. These loans can be risky for investors, because raw or significantly under-utilized land may not generate enough income to pay the interest on the loan. In this case, the interest may be pre-funded as part of the loan and set aside in an escrow account with the lender. If the property isn't sold or refinanced by the end of the loan, things can get ugly fast.

Construction Debt: Properties going through ground-up development have special loans designed specifically for developers. Usually the land and investor's cash is contributed first, then as further money is spent on approved expenses (such as site work, contractors, materials, etc.), the lender funds the construction loan in a series of "draws". Construction loans can be quite complex and time consuming for investors to administer. They are typically short term and structured to enable developers to go from entitled land to completed building as quickly as possible before refinancing or selling the property. Like land loans, the underlying properties often don't generate enough cash to service the debt.

Bridge Debt: Loans that are placed on properties going through significant transitions. Properties being mismanaged or properties that will go through a big renovation often don't fit well with perm lenders because they won't generate enough consistent cash flow to service perm debt. Bridge debt is used in these cases to allow the investor to execute on the business plan for the property, create value, kick-start cash flow, and then exit with a refinance or sale. Bridge loans are often floating rate, short-term loans with flexible prepayment structures.

Permanent ("Perm") Debt: Loans that are placed on stabilized properties with steady cash flow. Debt is usually sized based on property income and value and could be floating or fixed rate.

Loan Terms

Investors should be provided with loan terms, which you need to see to really understand an investment. Full loan quotes can be many pages long with an array of details about structures and terms, but the key terms to consider are the following:

Interest rate: The interest rate being charged annually on the outstanding loan balance. The rate can be either fixed or floating (a pre-defined spread over an index rate such as LIBOR, which is adjusted at regular intervals). Floaters usually have a floor rate, which is a minimum loan rate regardless of how far the index drops. Some lenders (life companies and some banks) use 30/360 payments, where monthly interest is calculated based on 30/360ths or 1/12th of a year each month… in other words, identical monthly payments. Other lenders (CMBS and agencies) tend to use actual/360 calculations where the actual number of days in the month are divided by 360 to calculate the monthly interest. Math wizzes amongst the readership will note that 360 is less than 365, meaning that actual 360 interest calculations are in practice a higher interest rate than the loan rate would indicate. This complexity, as is often the case, does not work in the favor of borrowers.

Amortization: The amount of principal being repaid during the loan term in addition to the interest being paid. This is described in terms of the number of years necessary to fully repay the loan. For example, a loan with 30-year amortization would take 30 years to repay.

Loan amount: The size of the loan being provided is unsurprisingly an important deciding factor for many borrowers. It is often constrained by a "lesser of" series of tests based on various underwriting criteria. For instance, a loan might be the lesser of $10,000,000, 70% loan-to-value, or the implied loan size based on a 1.25x debt-service-coverage. These underwriting tests are relevant to the lender, and also helpful for equity investors trying to understand a deal's risk profile. We will discuss them in more detail later in the book.

Term: The number of years before the loan must be repaid. The end of the loan term is the loan's maturity date. Unlike typical residential loans, CRE loans often have loan terms shorter than their amortization periods, which means although they may have partially paid down their principal balance, the borrower will need to pay the remainder (the balloon payment) at the end of the term. Balloon risk is the risk that the borrower won't be able to refinance the loan or sell the property and pay off the remaining loan balance.

Prepayment penalty: Unlike many residential mortgages, CRE loans are not necessarily prepayable without a penalty. The lowest prepayment penalties ("prepays") are usually on floating rate loans, which are often prepayable with no fee or a fixed (1%) fee. Fixed rate loans though, frequently include some type of penalty. The justification for this is that lenders are counting on the interest that would have been paid if the loan was not prepaid. As a result, yield maintenance (often associated with Fannie Mae or life company lenders) or defeasance (often associated with Freddie Mac or CMBS lenders) calculations are made that take into account both the remaining interest payable and prevailing interest rates when the loan is paid off. A quick online search will yield calculators that can estimate prepayment penalty amounts. Without going into the details, if interest rates go up, the prepayment penalty goes down, and vice versa. Life insurance companies and banks tend to be more flexible with prepayment penalties and will sometimes offer stepped-down prepays with decreasing penalties during the term of a loan. As an example, a 10-year loan might start out at a 5% prepayment penalty, then decrease by 1% every year until it reaches 1%, where it remains for the remainder of the term. Most loans have an open period at the end of their term without a prepayment penalty (often 90 days) providing the borrower with much needed flexibility to time the sale or refinance of their property without incurring costly penalties or going into default.

Escrows: Some properties have the potential for significant cash needs at some point in the future, and lenders need to consider these in advance. As an example, a new roof or a large lease expiration that necessitates spending for tenant improvements or leasing commissions may create risk for the lender (and the investors). Often, lenders may require an escrow, so money is set aside in advance to cover these potential costs from operating cash flow. If the cost isn't necessary (perhaps the large tenant renews their lease), the cash is distributed back to the partnership from the escrow account.

Other Fees: Lenders levy a blizzard of fees and expense reimbursements as part of the lending process, however the most material are usually the origination fees (fees in) and exit fees (fees out). Fees create another avenue for lenders to make money in addition to interest payments. The same amount of time and cost goes into underwriting and closing a loan regardless of how long the loan remains outstanding, so for shorter hold periods, these fees make up for the fact that lenders don't have much time to earn interest on their investment. Smaller and more complex loans usually have larger fees. Although they vary widely, 0.5% to 1.5% in and 0% to 1% out are in the realm of normal.

These are just a few of many key terms, but are generally the most important. As you might expect, lenders compete with various combinations of these terms and are willing to make tradeoffs between them or allow borrowers to pay extra to modify them.

When evaluating an offering, note the impact of the loan amortization schedule on the transaction. An amortizing loan requires the repayment of loan principal in addition to interest payments during the loan term. As a result, the loan balance decreases over time. The following chart shows the pace of loan balance repayment under typical amortization terms based on a 4% interest rate.

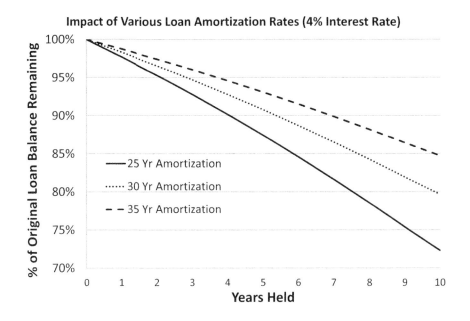

Amortization payments require extra cash, decreasing cash flow to investors and increasing the risk that the property will have cash flow shortfalls during the hold period – a potentially catastrophic problem. On the other hand, steady payments of loan principal decrease the unpaid principal balance due when the loan needs to be repaid, decreasing the risk that sale proceeds or refinance proceeds won't be sufficient to repay the lender. Lenders, of course, tend to prefer shorter amortization periods. For borrowers though, the impact of amortization is less clear. It increases operating risk but decreases exit risk. It decreases cash flow but increases proceeds upon a sale or refinance (in real estate parlance, a "capital event"). Based on a pure time-value-of-money analysis, it is always better to repay the loan later (slower amortization or more years of interest only) than sooner (faster amortization), but I tend to prefer slower amortization because it decreases default risk during the hold period.

Types of Lenders

There are a range of companies willing to provide mortgages to commercial real estate investors. Each has its own benefits, drawbacks, and quirks. There are three main items lenders consider when making a loan, 1) the value of the real estate, 2) the ability of the property to generate cash flow, and 3) the strength of the borrower. Different lenders have varying preferences about how to weigh the importance of these items, so they tend to be competitive on different deals. These are the sources you are likely to see frequently:

Banks: One of the most common lenders, banks lend money from their own balance sheet as part of a broadly diversified investment portfolio. Using balance sheet capital allows banks to be more flexible in nearly every way; lending on a variety of real estate (even outside the main food groups), having flexible prepayment penalties, and varying loan terms. Banks are also one of the more common lenders for construction loans or more complicated rehab loans where the lender funds a series of draws (post-close funding distributions) based on the completion of operational or physical requirements such as increases in NOI, leasing progress, or construction progress. Because banks are experienced lenders on all assets, they specialize in loans backed by both the real estate and personal recourse (a guarantee) from the borrower. In general, banks tend to be more competitive on short to medium term debt.

Life Insurance Companies: Life companies also invest money from their own balance sheets but generally have longer investment horizons and lower risk tolerances than banks. They specialize in low risk loans on higher quality real estate and often provide some of the least expensive financing available. They often service their own loans and have a reputation for being reasonable to work with in comparison to other lenders.

CMBS: Securitized lenders make loans temporarily funded through capital from their balance sheet, then bundle a portfolio of these loans together and sell them as a commercial mortgage backed security (CMBS) to other investors. The cash flow coming from this portfolio is sliced and diced in a dizzying array of ways to meet the unique needs of different investors. The details of the process are beyond the scope of this book, but as many readers are no doubt aware, the securitization of residential mortgages played a key part in the development of the financial crisis. The nuances of CMBS mean that loan underwriting tends to focus more on the real estate than the borrower, and lenders prefer properties with strong cash flow. CMBS loans are not usually the cheapest option, although they can be quite competitive at times, but they often provide some of the highest leverage available by senior lenders.   This means CMBS lenders are quite competitive on older vintage deals in secondary locations with weaker borrowers. After the loan closes, the securitization process often results in extremely clumsy and inflexible customer service with the borrower. CMBS lenders are notoriously difficult to deal with, sometimes purposefully, if something goes wrong and the loan defaults.

Agencies: In the multifamily world, Fannie Mae and Freddie Mac are large sources of mortgage capital. Although most people think of these agencies in the context of single-family home lending, they actively fund floating and fixed rate loans for apartment properties. Fannie and Freddie tend to finance mostly stabilized or value add properties rather than developments. The US Department of Housing and Urban Development (HUD) is also an active lender for apartment properties, and while painful to deal with, can provide very attractive 35 year fixed rate fully amortizing debt for borrowers with enough patience to go through the rigorous and byzantine application process. Whether, and to what extent, the agencies remain a fixture in multifamily lending is a constant source of industry debate and lobbying effort.   There is a reasonable chance that legislation could change the role of the agencies in the coming years, perhaps impacting the liquidity and value of multifamily properties for some time.

Hard Money / Loan Funds: A more eclectic group of lenders exists to handle all the loans that fall through the cracks between the primary lenders. Properties with environmental problems, extremely short closing timelines (days sometimes), no cash flow, unusual specialty uses, or other attributes that add risk for lenders, might still be a fit for these groups. Fees and rates for hard money loans are expensive and leverage tends to be low, but they often make sense for borrowers with an extraordinary opportunity and no other options. Because of the higher returns, these funds are sometimes popular with private investors who are willing to take on (or unaware of) the extra risk involved. Although the returns are materially higher than other fixed income investments, these funds can fail spectacularly when the real estate market stumbles.

Overall, the lending market is surprisingly efficient, but it is critical to make sure you are getting quotes from the right lender for each deal. Because preferences change quickly (usually as annual allocations are filled up), it can be challenging for smaller borrowers to know who to be speaking with and to have the leverage to negotiate the best deal. Commercial mortgage brokers are valuable in these cases, using their market knowledge to help borrowers find the best lender and negotiate the best deal. Perhaps technology will limit the value of this specialty over time, but for the moment mortgage brokers are an important part of the system.

Detailed information about the loan should be standard information disclosed during the offering process and should definitely be taken into account when evaluating deals. While passive investors have little recourse beyond not participating if they don't like terms, lenders are risk averse, so reviewing some of their metrics (which we discuss in more detail later in the book) can be an excellent way of gauging risk to equity investors. After all, if the lender is losing money, equity investors have usually been wiped out. If lenders have legitimate reasons to be wary of a deal, equity investors should be aware that there is major risk involved with their investment.

C) Subordinate Debt

Subordinate debt, aka "junior" or "mezzanine"/"mezz" debt, is a higher leverage slice of debt that slips into the capital structure between the senior debt and the equity. By between, we are describing the priority of who receives cash being distributed from the deal. The senior lender has first priority on being paid, then the subordinate lender, then the common equity.

The basic mechanics of mezz debt are simple - it acts just like senior debt when things are going well. At closing, the mezz lender funds cash into escrow to capitalize the property acquisition. The borrower pays the mezz lender interest during the loan term and repays the remaining balance at the end of the term. Like senior debt, mezz often has loan fees and prepayment penalties if it is paid off early.

To illustrate, let's go through a quick example. A property is purchased for $10,000,000. A 70% LTV loan ($7,000,000) is provided by a senior lender. A mezzanine lender provides one third of the remaining capital needed, 10% ($1,000,000), which takes the combined LTV up to 80% ($8,000,000 of combined proceeds). The remaining 20% of the capitalization ($2,000,000) is funded with equity.

While the property is operating normally, the senior lender receives a 4.5% fixed interest-only payment ($315,000 annually) and the mezzanine lender receives a 12% fixed interest-only payment ($120,000 annually). The common equity gets all distributions left over, if any, after the combined $435,000 annual payment is made to the senior lender and the preferred equity. The combined payment is a blended 5.44% rate.

When the property is sold or refinanced, the cash is distributed in order of priority. If mezz loans have the same maturity date as the senior loan, they are described as being "coterminous", a situation that can make planning a sale or refinance simpler for the borrower. Let's assume the senior lender and the preferred equity have both been paid current, which means they have received their interest or preferred return so far. If that case, first the senior lender is repaid its $7,000,000, then the mezz lender is repaid its $1,000,000, then any remaining cash is distributed to the equity holders.

In practice, adding mezz debt to a capital stack introduces a wealth of complexity to a transaction. While some lenders will provide both the senior and the mezz debt, for mechanical reasons that aren't worth going into, usually the senior and mezz lender are different groups. Mezz lenders tend to be smaller entrepreneurial shops (often private funds) rather than large institutions and are often more flexible and daring than their stodgier senior lending brethren.

Mezz lenders, like senior lenders, have strong rights to foreclose and/or take over operational control of a property if a borrower is in monetary default (has missed a payment) or in technical default (has failed one of a variety of performance tests or legal requirements described in the loan documents). Reputations and strategies vary widely in the industry from lenders who have no interest in taking back real estate to those who are hoping something goes awry so they will have an opportunity to take over a property at a discount through foreclosure.

Loans from mezz lenders earn a significantly higher rate of interest than senior debt, often two or three times as much. While this might seem exorbitant, think back to the earlier graphic describing the pricing of debt. Keep in mind that risk increases exponentially as leverage increases. Furthermore, mezz lenders are only holding the riskiest strip of debt in the capital stack – their money is only slightly senior to equity, so they require returns high enough to compensate them for this risk. Despite these higher rates, the overall cost of debt including senior and junior lenders (the blended rate) is often only slightly higher than the rate of the senior loan because the amount of mezz debt is usually much smaller than the amount of senior debt.

D) Preferred Equity

Preferred equity, aka "pref equity" or "PE" is not quite debt but not quite equity. Debt is generally an investment that receives a fixed return but no upside, whereas equity is an investment that involves no guarantees or preference but has the potential for unlimited upside if a deal does well. Preferred equity is a bit of a soup, mixing together pieces of each.

Like mezz, PE slips into the capital stack between senior debt and common equity. Also, like mezz, PE receives a fixed yield (a "preferred return" or "pref") that is subordinate to the senior lender. Once the pref has been paid, any remaining distributions are split between the preferred equity and the common equity. These equity splits can become relatively complicated waterfall structures, which are described in more detail in the next chapter. To offset the fact that preferred equity shares in potential upside, the preferred return is usually lower than the interest rate that would be charged by a mezzanine lender providing the same amount of capital.

As you can see, although PE and mezz investments sit in the same place in the capital structure, they are economically very different. Each has benefits and drawbacks for the lender and the borrower, and neither is inherently more risky than the other.

To illustrate, let's go through another quick example analogous to our prior mezz debt scenario. A property is purchased for $10,000,000. A 70% LTV loan ($7,000,000) is provided by a senior lender. A preferred equity investor provides half of the remaining capital needed; 15% ($1,500,000), which takes the combined LTV up to 85%. The remaining 15% of capitalization ($1,500,000) is funded with common equity.

While the property is operating normally, the senior lender receives a 4.5% fixed interest-only payment ($315,000 annually). The preferred equity investor receives an 8% pref ($120,000 annually), after which it receives 20% of any remaining distributions. The common equity gets 80% of any distributions left over after the combined $435,000 annual payment is made to the senior lender and the preferred equity. The combined payment is a blended 5.12% rate.

When the property is sold or refinanced, the proceeds are split between the parties. Let's assume the senior lender and the preferred equity have both been paid current. The senior lender is paid back their $7,000,000 first, then the preferred equity is repaid its initial $1,500,000 investment, then the common equity is repaid its initial $1,500,000 investment. Any remaining cash is split 20% to the preferred equity and 80% to the common equity.

This is a typical structure, but the reality of preferred equity is that nothing is standard. Because it is not really equity and not really debt, it is often a custom-made investment designed specifically to fit the nuances of a particular property and operator. Still, when things go south, it gets ugly for everyone. As a result, lenders don't like either mezzanine debt or preferred equity in a deal if they can help it, and they often charge borrowers a premium or impose other restrictions if these additional structures are used if they don't outright prohibit them. Of the two, lenders usually prefer PE investments because they share attributes of equity and don't always immediately enter default (and trigger foreclosure and litigation) if a payment is missed.

Because everything is negotiable, PE investors try to make their investments act as much like mezzanine debt as possible (giving them more leverage if things don't go well), without actually calling it that. This adds cost, complexity, and uncertainty into deals. One of the most difficult and complicated transactions I have had the displeasure of being involved with from the sponsor side was a portfolio of properties being capitalized with a senior lender and preferred equity. The entire transaction was a three way negotiation between the lender's counsel (who prohibited mezzanine debt and wanted the preferred equity agreement to act like common equity), the preferred equity investor's counsel (who wanted to the preferred equity to act like mezzanine debt with a different name), and us (we sided with the senior lender but really just wanted to get the deal closed). The moral of the story, for me, was that you should never need to use complicated structured products. If they make sense and add value to your unique deal, by all means make use of them. But using them purely to juice investment returns is probably not a good long-term investment strategy.

Evaluating the Capital Structure

As a potential investor, you should think in advance about the amount and types of risk you are willing to accept due to financial structuring, and where you would like to invest in the capital stack. Although most people associate real estate investing with equity ownership, as an investor in private offerings there are opportunities to participate in all parts of the capital stack, tailoring investments to meet your unique investment goals and risk profile. Investments in common equity, debt, mezz debt, and pref equity all have their own benefits and drawbacks and none are inherently good or bad. Think about what profile matches your investment targets and risk tolerance, then look for investments fitting those criteria.

Using debt in the capital structure magnifies equity investment returns, making good deals better and bad deals worse. The more debt is used, the higher the magnification. At least on paper, more debt usually means higher underwritten returns, but investors would be wise to consider the potential risk in high leverage deals. A bad financing strategy can completely implode an otherwise fine real estate deal. The real estate world is full of borrower tales of woe about otherwise good deals given back to the lender before the investor's grand plans could be realized. Some of these tales might even be true. On the other hand, rare is the poor investment that is saved by a great loan. Bad investments usually suck sooner and later.

As an equity investor, the terms of debt, mezzanine, or preferred equity financing should be clearly described so you can understand exactly what risk you're bearing. I personally tend to shy away from complicated and highly leveraged deals after seeing so many of them in distress as soon as the economy and real estate market dips – something that has been known to happen from time to time. Managers love leverage because it increases upside and the potential to earn promotes, something we will discuss later. Investors like the higher pro forma returns underwritten with higher leverage. Lenders and other providers of structured products make their living earning fees from providing these types of capital. Everyone is happy... until they aren't. Keep it simple and look for good real estate and managers that add real value rather than creating it artificially, and temporarily, through complicated capital structures.

CHAPTER 3: EVALUATING THE SPONSOR

*"The human story does not always unfold like a mathematical calculation...
[T]he element of the unexpected and the unforeseeable is what gives some of its
relish and saves us from falling into the mechanical thralldom of the logicians." –
Winston Churchill*

The lack of control inherent in passive investments is both a blessing and a curse for investors. Because the GP controls, or at the very least, influences every major decision related to the partnership, investors need to pick their managers with care. It's easy to focus on quantitative factors when reviewing potential investments. Investing is not just about projected returns though, which are mostly just storytelling anyway. Even the best real estate can't overcome the damage caused by a bad operator. Investors are well served by setting aside pro forma returns and development budgets to focus on the people driving the business. If I had the choice between evaluating only the manager or the real estate before making an investment, I would choose the manager every time. The relationship between managers and investors is a symbiotic partnership, so take care to pick your partner well - you will be stuck with them for a long time! You want an experienced, motivated, and capable group making decisions on your behalf.

Despite being perhaps the most important aspect of your investment, actually evaluating managers can be tough in practice. Assessing managers is a messy and imprecise process, sort of like interviewing potential employees. The best way to get a sense of the performance and character of a manager is to have long term experience with them, through good times and bad. Therefore, referrals to managers through trusted friends or advisers are extremely valuable.

Don't be afraid to set up a meeting in person to talk through the company's investment strategy and infrastructure. Ideally, meet at the company's offices so you can see the operation in person and get a better sense of the scale and scope of the group. It is hard to beat sitting down and speaking face to face with someone to evaluate their dedication and passion for their craft. Although most companies will accommodate these meetings, be respectful of their time – the economics of real estate mean that most companies are thinly staffed. For those with many smaller private investors, spending big chunks of time with each investor can take away from the everyday blizzard of tasks necessary to find and manage deals on behalf of all their investors. Some companies have dedicated investor relations teams, and some don't.

You might be able to find a reference by asking around, particularly with very locally focused operators, but sometimes this just isn't practical. Thankfully, basic information about the manager is always available as part of the offering materials or upon request. One of the key pieces of information to evaluate is the manager's investment track record. Usually this is provided as a list of properties purchased, including property name, location, purchase/sale dates, net LP returns, and some simple property information. Hopefully, the manager has been around long enough to show a significant history of sold deals, or "round trips". Obviously, it's good to see high average returns to investors, but this is only one factor to consider. Dig in a bit more to see how volatile their returns are and if they have had any complete losses. Are their averages skewed up or down by a few outliers? Consider the vintage (year purchased) of their transactions to fairly evaluate them. It is a good sign if managers slowed their deal volume or sat out from the market during times of market froth so they could wait for better opportunities.

Look for consistency of product type, market, and investment strategy across the history of the manager, and make sure they have sufficient experience relevant to the deal you are considering. Each product type and market has its own unique issues to deal with. It is better for the GP's education not to come at the expense of your investment. Setting aside the actual execution after closing, this expertise is also important because most sellers and brokers gravitate toward buyers who have extensive experience matching their deal as a way to minimize their own transaction risk. Having a reputation for on-point deal experience and being reasonable to work with are critical to being on the short list of potential buyers being contacted for off-market or limited-market deals. In other words, having relevant experience is necessary to be able to negotiate attractive purchase prices. Lacking experience and reputation, the only way to differentiate yourself as a buyer is to pay more than everyone else, which isn't a proven winning strategy in real estate.

The next important factor to evaluate is the executive team. Most well-rounded investment companies need an experienced team with expertise in investments, accounting, operations, construction, property and asset management, and possibly human resources. The depth of the executive team is crucial to successful deal sourcing, purchasing, and post-close execution. Review the biographies provided for senior executives, looking for relevant industry experience, tenure at the company, and transaction volume. Acquisitions people should know their industry counterparts and have closed many similar deals, management people should have overseen similar properties to know how to deal with operational nuances, and accounting people should have enough relevant experience to reliably oversee the books and coordinate with auditors or partners. Ideally, the executive team will have worked together for a long time, minimizing risk from new processes and from key employee turnover.

For smaller transactions, not every operator has a fully integrated platform. This can be manageable because nearly every function can be outsourced to a vendor and the real estate world has a wealth of excellent service providers for small companies. In these cases, a clear plan should be in place for the operation of the property throughout the planned investment horizon, and the third parties involved should have the experience necessary to handle the deal. There are benefits and drawbacks to outsourcing parts of the business process. Some companies use their in-house systems as a competitive advantage to provide them with real-time market data and excellent service. Other companies are inefficient fee-hogs and their investors would be better served by hiring industry experts for property management or accounting.

If a company doesn't have a 30-year track record, don't dismiss them immediately. At least hear the pitch. Great new companies are formed all the time, and truly creative and differentiated strategies can be hard to execute in the confines of an existing successful company. Real estate investing can be hard enough on its own though, so don't take on more platform risk than you need to, and watch out for small shops that need to do deals just to keep the fees rolling in and the lights on.

Conflicts of Interest

Because of the complicated set of incentives typical to real estate transactions, which are discussed more in the "Compensation & Fees" chapter, it is nearly impossible to avoid conflicts of interest between managers and investors. For fully integrated investment companies with multiple partnerships and sources of equity, conflicts of interest are unavoidable.

Fees or compensation to related entities is one of the most common sources of conflicts. As an example, let's take property management. In this case, ACME Real Estate is a GP who has syndicated a real estate deal. ACME sets up a separate but related entity, ACME Management, to provide property management services. ACME Management is paid a property management fee of 3% by the limited partnership that owns the real estate. As the GP, ACME Real Estate determines what it should pay itself (through ACME Management) as a fee. This fee is typically not an arms-length negotiation and is often above the going rate for property management services available from third party providers. This is a common situation and one that may or may not be good for investors. ACME Management, due to its relationship to ACME Real Estate, is likely to do a better job managing the deal than a third-party property manager. The unfortunate reality of property management is that contracts are often awarded to low-cost leaders since evaluating property management quality is notoriously difficult and comparing fees is easy. To complicate the situation, ACME Management has a relatively small management portfolio, making it less efficient than large third-party commodity managers. As a result, this above-market property management fee may be around break-even for ACME Management, but worth doing to add value to the holdings of ACME Real Estate.

In my experience, this example is not particularly unusual, although some companies take the opportunity to create large profit centers from fees paid to related entities, and these fees have the potential to create a large hidden drag on investment returns for their partners. Worse, managers may be incentivized not to sell properties to keep the fees rolling in or to delay the sale of a property to avoid damaging their track record by recognizing a loss. You can see how convoluted these potential conflicts of interest can become. Private placement memorandums ("PPMs"), discussed more later, include a detailed section on potential conflicts of interest, describing in excruciating detail every possible conflict. The following section "Compensation & Fees" includes further discussion on fees and conflicts of interest. In general though, investors nearly always have to rely on GPs to manage a wide variety of conflicts of interest as a regular course of business. This is an unfortunate reality in the industry and adds to the importance of choosing trustworthy managers.

CHAPTER 4:
COMPENSATION & FEES

"It is difficult to get a man to understand something, when his salary depends upon his not understanding it!" – Upton Sinclair

This chapter is about compensation; what LPs pay GPs for the privilege of participating in their offerings. People don't work for free, so real estate companies need to be compensated. There are two basic ways GP compensation is structured:

1. Fees: Compensation paid to the GP regardless of performance. Fees incentivize GPs to do deals. Lots of deals… any deals! The more deals they do, the more they make.

2. Performance-based compensation: Payments to the GP that occur only if an investment goes well. This type of comp is easier to sell to investors, because it appears to align incentives by motivating GPs to pick good deals over bad deals. In reality, a moderately efficient market (discussed more later) means that returns are related to risk, so performance-based comp has the unintended consequence of motivating GPs to do riskier deals.

Both types of compensation obviously have benefits and drawbacks. Investors would like GPs' incentives to be perfectly aligned with their own, but this is impossible. Most compensation is structured as a combination of the first and second alternatives above, which at least avoids the extremes of misalignment. We will go through the most common terms so you can understand how compensation is occurring on any given transaction, evaluate aggregate compensation to understand if it is reasonable, and recognize the mix of incentives being created.

Before delving into the details of terms, let's divert briefly to talk about how real estate investment companies make money in theory and in practice. Expenses first. Expense structures depend on how vertically integrated a company is. A small real estate company might consist of one person, an executive suite, a cell phone, and a laptop. These companies are nimble and have the able to quickly jump on market opportunities as they present themselves. Without much overhead, small companies don't require much cash to operate, but because of their limited scope of services they have few sources of cash to maintain even these limited operations. This is a common profile for startup companies that may need to keep doing deals and earning fees just to pay the founder's mortgage.

On the other end of the spectrum are full service real estate investment and management companies. These owner/operators employ the full range of employees and provide a variety of services; accounting and reporting, investment services, capital markets (equity raising and debt), property and asset management, construction oversight, and human resources. These are big complex machines with a lot of inertia and operational expenses to pay regardless of market conditions or the availability of good investment opportunities. They can't simply close up shop for a year or two while they wait for the market to return to equilibrium and then pick up where they left off. As a result, they tend to be in markets on the way up and on the way down and rely on relationships and execution to manage through market cycles.

I have experienced the pleasure and pain of working for both types of organizations and don't feel strongly that one is inherently better than the other. Smaller companies tend to be spry, with the ability to chase opportunities based on unique market conditions. Bigger companies use their reputation, relationships, and track record to their advantage to source and control deals within their area of specialization.

Both types of companies make money by earning (or at least charging) fees for services and through performance-based incentives. The combination of the two needs to cover overhead during lean times and provide a reward for the capital and time invested by partners in organizing deals. Some investors push hard for fees to be minimal and for GP compensation to be highly incentive based. I think this is a big mistake, one that causes excessive risk taking; an issue we will discuss more later. Each manager has its own unique recipe for compensation, making direct comparisons hard. Rather than focus on each individual term, investors are better served by reviewing them in bulk and deciding if the compensation is reasonable in total and if incentives are relatively well aligned. You might expect strong sponsors with great track records to be able to charge the highest fees/promotes and startup sponsors to have lower compensation to draw investors to their deals, but that isn't necessarily the case in my experience. If anything, the opposite is true, with small syndicators charging big loads on small deals, a sure recipe for long-term underperformance. Crowdfunded deals in particular seem to be fee hogs, at least in the current marketplace. If you can pay the same or lower load to invest with an industry veteran, why wouldn't you?

Often vertically integrated firms will handle more services in-house and charge investors for those services while smaller groups will outsource the same services. Either way the partnership is being charged; make sure you take internal and external fees into account when comparing small shops to large operations to ensure you are making a fair comparison. As a simple test, look at the difference between the underlying real estate returns (with no fees or promote) and the net LP returns (including all fees and promote) to get a sense of the size of the total drag on your investment. This can be complicated because the load can vary depending on the performance of a deal, but it is a quick way to see how much investors are paying the GP for its services.

Capital allocators are companies that raise money from investors, then invest it as a major investor or joint-venture investor with other real estate investment companies rather than directly purchase and operate real estate. Many comingled real estate funds fall into this category as well as many offerings by money management companies. As discussed earlier, many of these groups add significant value for investors by finding transactions, negotiating attractive terms, and overseeing the GP's execution. Others... don't. These groups are compensated with fees and promotes as well as the GPs for each deal, creating the potential for investors to pay a double promote. When investing into this type of structure, keep in mind that everyone involved needs to be paid, and the more layers of groups involved, the faster the fees add up and the more you are diluted.

The restrictions on public offerings make industry-wide comparisons of deal terms nearly impossible. A few groups of investors have tried to aggregate deal terms and track records with varying levels of success. GPs are limited in most cases from widely distributing offerings, which is fine with them. Fees and terms are your product's price; why advertise your pricing to competitors? This alignment of regulations and natural business discretion has created a "Bootleggers and Baptists" type of coalition, resulting in a surprisingly inefficient market for offerings; terms are opaque, vary widely between companies, and contain plenty of manager discretion over when and how they might be applied and interpreted. While there are limits on distribution, the GP community is small so it's not uncommon to have an opportunity to review competitors' offerings and it's normal to use these as a benchmark, particularly when companies' investor groups overlap. There is no such thing as a set of "standard" terms, but over time you will get a sense of what's normal and what's egregious.

Fees

Here is a quick summary of the most common types of fees, along with the usual justification for the charge and typical amounts. This summary is based on my own experience reading and writing many private offerings but is by no means comprehensive or universal.

Acquisition Fees

Investors hate acquisition fees. Even so, as one of the primary sources of fee income for investment companies they are here to stay. Acquisition fees are typically earned upon acquisition of a property and paid when it closes. For GPs who invest material equity in their deals, these fees offset their cash contribution. This is often described as being paid a fee in equity. In cases with small or no GP co-invest, these fees may be paid out in cash. While there are some justifications for it, I usually view a cash-out acquisition fee as a red flag that the GP is too highly incentivized to prefer deal volume over deal quality.

There are legitimate reasons for acquisition fees to exist. GPs invest serious time and money getting a transaction closed, not to mention being on the hook for "busted deal costs" - pursuit costs for deals that never close. They risk their own money, often seven figures, for temporary transaction deposits while properties are under contract. They take on full, partial, or carve-out recourse for mortgages (described more later); meaning that while LPs may lose their entire investment, GPs may lose their entire investment in the property and be liable for further losses to the lender. Lastly, performance incentives aren't paid until properties are sold, which could be 10 or more years after acquisition. Acquisition fees can provide cash either directly or through operating distributions to fund company operations and pursue new transactions in the meantime.

Acquisition fees are usually quoted as a percentage of the purchase price of a property. 1% is common, anything below around 2% is within a normal range. Pay attention to the total dollar size of the fees as well as the percentage; smaller transactions may be just as costly and difficult to execute so can justify higher percentage fees.

Disposition fees

Like acquisition fees, disposition fees are much maligned by investors. Perhaps they have more of a point here because some of the justifications for acquisition fees simply don't apply to disposition fees. Selling properties is far less work organizationally than buying properties, with much of the heavy lifting being done by brokers who are hired by and paid for by the partnership. There are no loans to be arranged or equity to be raised.

Perhaps it is better to think about disposition fees as a slight tweak to the cash waterfall (discussed more shortly) upon sale, wherein the GP takes a small 100% distribution before the remainder of the waterfall kicks in. In fact, some disposition fees are tied to performance (for instance, only paid of the preferred return is met) in which case they are more of a catch-up tier in the waterfall than a fee.

Regardless, they are not unusual or particularly objectionable as part of a well-rounded transaction. Expect fees to be paid as a percentage of the property sale price, often at or below the percentage of the acquisition fee.

Financing (or Refinancing) Fees

Although occasional, financings and refinancings can be time consuming for staff and go above and beyond the normal course of asset management or property management duties. Some loans, such as HUD debt for multifamily properties, can take more than a year to process and involve a relentless barrage of meetings, reports, and negotiation. Larger groups will have an internal team dedicated to arranging debt and managing the process, and their ongoing relationships and transaction volume may mean they can negotiate more attractive terms for a partnership, adding value to the property. Alternatively, smaller groups may engage third party mortgage bankers to manage financing relationships.

Financing fees are typically no higher than 1% of the loan balance and drop to around 0.5% or less for larger loans. Not all GPs take this fee, it is usually justified to support an in-house financing team. Ask if an external group will be engaged because fees to bankers combined with fees to the GP can quickly become material.

Equity placement fees

Equity placement fees

Placement fees are paid to an internal or external sales team responsible for raising equity for a transaction or fund. Fees are often around 2% to 3%, but can be much higher. Keep in mind that salespeople are paid to sell deals, not to sell good deals. Some companies have good strategic reasons for growing their capital base quickly; perhaps they are scaling a syndication business into a fund business or they are a startup with deal flow but few investor relationships. Other companies are sales machines for whom any deal that can be done is a deal worth doing. Each deal is a fee in the bank and an option on a promote. Equity placement fees aren't a non-starter, but it's preferable to see operators raise equity organically through a steady transaction pipeline and positive word of mouth.

If fees are paid, ask if they are paid by the individual investor or the partnership. Because they are essentially sales commissions, they may not apply to all investors and GPs often have discretion about how they are levied. They are one of the rare fees where individual investors may be able to negotiate a more attractive deal for themselves. If larger groups of investors qualify for lower fees, ask to be included in those groups.

Expense Reimbursements

Because of the timing of the transaction process, GPs often need to pay expenses out of pocket with the expectation that they will be reimbursed at or after closing. This is nearly always done as a direct reimbursement with no markup. Typical reimbursements are not too controversial if the expenses apply directly to the transaction and are for the benefit of all investors. Legal, organizational and offering (O&O), transaction deposits, lender deposits, due diligence, and third-party reports are all very common reimbursements, many of which are paid or reimbursed to the GP at closing.

Things get trickier for some other categories of expenses. Equity placement fees are sometimes included under O&O expenses and paid by the partnership. If all investors are paying the same load, this doesn't create any conflicts between investors, although this cost is sometimes borne by the GP directly without reimbursement. In situations where some partners invest directly and others invest through intermediaries (who are paid a fee), if the expense is paid by the fund or partnership, direct investors could be bearing some of the costs paid to raise equity from others; often an objectionable prospect.

Related Entity Reimbursements or Payments

Vertically integrated companies perform services that smaller companies may need to outsource to third parties. As discussed on the section on conflicts of interests, this is often great for investors. Having a true owner's perspective on property operations and asset management issues brings an attentiveness to detail and decision-making rigor that arms-length parties rarely have.

Also, it's harder to measure effectiveness with third party groups, so they are often selected based on cost and might be less likely to spend money to make money. Although everyone understands that the goal should be to maximize NOI, separating the contributions of operations and market trends on revenue is extremely difficult. By comparison, it's easy to see how operational decisions drive expenses.

Having an ongoing source of operational fee income helps ensure that GPs can continue to operate their portfolio even when the market turns for the worse and the pipeline of new transactions shuts down. A GP in financial distress isn't in anyone's best interest!

Although there are benefits to self-management, it's not always better for owners to operate their own properties. Smaller groups may not have the scale to efficiently operate properties. Spreading fixed costs over a small portfolio might still be too costly in comparison to hiring a large third-party management company.

In situations where companies or a related party earn fees from ongoing operations, it's important to understand if their charges are reasonable in comparison to the costs of hiring a third party. You also need to know how the expenses are allocated across the company's portfolio to ensure that some properties aren't being subsidized by others. As discussed previously with financing fees, make sure the GP isn't being paid for services that are also being provided by third parties.

GP Co-Invest

A "co-invest" refers to the amount of equity the GP owns in a transaction and is usually described as a percentage of the deal's total equity. LPs usually prefer to see larger co-invests because it shows that the GP has more skin in the game. Putting house money at risk is a very effective way to demonstrate conviction in an investment.

In bigger transactions or funds where the total equity requirement is large, it is not usual for the co-invest to be a set dollar amount or to be capped. The justification for this is usually that if a GP has, say, $1,000,000 in a transaction, they will care about the outcome regardless of the equity percentage this represents. While this might be true, $1,000,000 means different things to different people, and LPs shouldn't count on this alone to ensure interests are aligned.

Often upfront fees are contributed to the transaction as partial or full consideration toward the GP co-invest. Normally LPs prefer to see GPs contribute some meaningful new cash to a transaction in addition to a contribution of fees. Economists would probably argue that the source of the equity is irrelevant, but most LPs I know disagree.

Although some smaller operators do not contribute a co-invest (or even take cash fees out of transactions upfront – yikes!), most GPs co-invest around 5%-10% of each deal's equity. For larger deals or funds, this may drop to 1%-2% or be capped at $1,000,000 to $2,000,000, but these are usually negotiated on an individual basis and depend on a variety of circumstances, not the least of which is the GP's capacity to invest.

Incentive Compensation

The next type of compensation is probably the most misunderstood, even by sophisticated investors. "Carried Interest" or a "Promote" is a performance incentive where the GP receives extra money when the deal does well. The yardstick to measure performance is usually the investment's internal rate of return ("IRR" or compounded return) but could also be based on a non-compounded return or an investment multiple.

Waterfalls

We should take a short detour at this point to go over the concept of a waterfall. A waterfall is a sequential series of rules defining how cash from a transaction is distributed. These structures and descriptions can be extremely complex, but usually have some similarities. Let's go through a simplified example, something you might see in typical offering documents:

1. First, 100% of cash goes to LPs, until LPs have received an 8% IRR
2. Then, 80% of cash goes to LPs, and 20% of cash goes to the GP until the LPs have received a 15% IRR
3. Then, 60% of cash goes to LPs, and 40% of cash goes to the GP

To understand this waterfall, you can visualize the distributions from a property as a stream of dollars/water flowing from a hose (or a very small waterfall). The first dollars from the stream flow into an empty bucket. They keep flowing into the bucket until it fills up, which is when the preferred return (8% in our example) is met. At this point, dollars/water pour over the side into the second bucket, which fills up until the next hurdle is met (15% in our example). When the second bucket is full, water pours into the last bucket. Since this is the last level of our waterfall, this bucket is infinitely big, so all remaining distributions can fit in the last bucket.

Once all distributions are complete and have flowed into the appropriate bucket, the dollars/water is distributed between the parties.

1. All the money in our first bucket is distributed according to the rules in level #1 of our waterfall above. In our example, all money is distributed to LPs. Unless otherwise described, distributions to LPs are usually made according to their ownership percentage (sometimes called pro-rata). So a partner who owns 10% of a property will receive 10% of distributions from this part of the waterfall.

2. The second bucket is split according to waterfall level #2: 20% to the GP, and the remaining 80% to the LPs pro rata.

3. The last bucket is split according to waterfall level #3: 40% to the GP, and the remaining 60% to the LPs pro rata.

See the following graphic for an intricate visual rendering of this process.

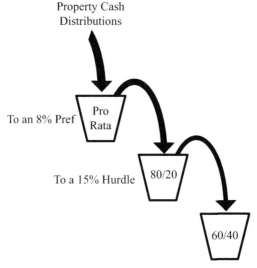

An Example Waterfall

Depending on the size of the co-invest, the GP may be a significant owner of LP interests. Most promotes are designed so the GP receives the promote in addition to their portion of any distributions to LPs. For example, a GP receiving a 20% promote who has a 10% LP interest will receive:

$$Promote\ (20\%) + LP\ Interest\ (10\%\ of\ 80\%) = 28\%\ of\ cash\ flow$$

The key to understanding a waterfall is that the split for each step only applies to the cash being distributed in that step. Unlike many hedge funds or other alternative investments with much lower or non-existent preferred returns, equity real estate preferred returns are often around 8% -12%, although this varies with other terms. As a result, investment returns on moderately performing deals may not be diluted as much as you might think because not much cash ends up in any of the promoted buckets.

If you are scanning documents and want to do some napkin-math to estimate how much the promote will dilute your returns, I find it easier to start with a hypothetical property-level investment return, then add up the cumulative promote in each stage of the waterfall and subtract it from your total return. To demonstrate this, let's assume a 20% deal level IRR and use our example waterfall:

1. No promote from 0% to 8%
2. 20% promote from 8% to 15% (20% of 7%) = 1.4% loss
3. 40% promote from 15% to 20% (40% of 5%) = 2.0% loss

$$20\% \ (Property \ IRR) - 1.4\% - 2.0\% = 17.6\% \ (Net \ LP \ IRR)$$

This gives you a quick way to estimate the load caused by the GP's promote. Don't worry about being too precise here. The goal is to get a general feel for how much you're being diluted and to decide if you think it's reasonable given all the other fees involved and the quality of the deal. Despite the pages of complex spreadsheets attached to the offering, forecasting returns is a total crap shoot. Don't sweat the details calculating this return, it's more important to know if it's reasonable compared to other offerings.

Catch-Ups

A catch-up is a special level added to a waterfall that gives the GP a large portion of distributions until they "catch up" to a target split. This is really just a special case of the more general waterfall levels described above, but it's common enough and material enough to warrant discussion.

If you look carefully, you can find catch-ups in the wild, hiding in their own level of the waterfall behind language like this: "100% of distributions to GP until GP has received 20% of cumulative distributions." Sounds innocuous, right? Is that really so different than having an 80/20 split? Yes: let's look at a quick example, comparing this to the waterfall above. To keep it simple, we will pick a scenario where the GP has completed the catch up (10%) and use our quick dilution calculation from above:

Example waterfall:
1. No promote from 0% to 8%
2. 20% promote from 8% to 10% (20% of 2%) = 0.4% loss

$$10\% \ (property \ IRR) - 0.4\% = 9.6\% \ Net \ LP \ IRR$$

Example waterfall with catch-up:
1. No promote from 0% to 8%
2. 100% promote from 8% to 10% (100% of 2%) = 2.0% loss

$$10\% \ (property \ IRR) - 2.0\% = \ 8.0\% \ Net \ LP \ IRR$$

Even in this very modestly returning deal, the catch-up alone results in a 1.6% IRR dilution - pretty material. This alone would not necessarily be bad if the rest of the fees and structure were LP friendly enough to make up for the economic loss of the catch up. My real discomfort with catch-ups though, goes beyond the dilution and involves the misalignment of interest they create between GPs and LPs. Promotes by their nature distort incentives, but catch ups do so in an extreme way that can incentivize GPs to take more risk or hold properties longer than they should based on the underlying real estate investment fundamentals.

Many catch-ups use a lower split (50/50 is common too), which helps, but still creates some weird incentives.   Other fees are sometimes triggered if investments hit a preferred return and while they are usually smaller in magnitude, they can also create misalignments of interest. These structures are well intentioned, and probably even do some good by avoiding "fee hog" GP business models, but they can create a hidden cost to LPs when they influence the decision to hold or sell a property in a way that doesn't maximize property level returns.

Fund Terms

Syndicates and funds have quite a bit of overlap in terms, but the co-mingled, blind pool nature of funds creates some unique issues that simple single-deal syndications don't need to deal with.

Closings, Capital Calls, and Fundraising

Because the fundraising process for blind pool funds commonly takes upwards of six to twelve months or more to finish, GPs have to carefully manage both the investment and the fundraising processes in parallel, investing capital before the fund is fully subscribed and closed. If they waited for a final closing, early investors would have to stay liquid (sit on cash that's not earning a meaningful return) for up to a year after committing to the fund. Investors don't like doing that, so funds avoid it.

Instead, when a fund reaches a minimum level of commitments, it starts making investments and drawing down equity as needed. This minimum level is usually set to be large enough that the fund could fulfil its investment strategy and continue to operate if no more money were raised. As more investors commit and more properties are acquired, additional cash is called from investors.

This is not an ideal scenario, because later investors have an advantage over earlier investors – they know at least some of the deals in the fund and may even have preliminary indications of their performance. As a result, fundraising starts slow while LPs take a wait-and-see approach to the offering, hoping to jump in at the last minute depending on how the process unfolds.

To manage this problem, preferred deal terms sometimes exist for early investors or a large seed investor who commits early in exchange for favorable treatment. This is a fair way to compensate early investors for the additional risk, but the underlying problem remains.

As you review fund offerings, make sure the first closing is large enough to have critical mass, and look for a limit on final closings in a reasonable amount of time after that. If you are an early investor, ask if you get preferred terms.

As we just discussed, most funds are designed so capital is called by the GP as needed to fund transactions. As an example, two weeks before a scheduled acquisition, LPs would be informed that they need to fund their pro-rata portion of the equity for an acquisition within a 10-day time frame. If funds aren't contributed within the required window, it can complicate the transaction for the GP, who may need to scramble to fund equity for a deal. As a result, there are often penalties assessed or other disincentives for non-contributing LPs. The clock used to calculate the preferred return and IRR calculations starts ticking when equity is contributed, which means that although LPs may commit to an investment, they could have to sit on liquid assets that aren't earning much of a return, until deals are found.

Not all funds are set up this way; some ask for contributions immediately when investors commit to the fund and LPs start earning a preferred return right away. Some investors prefer this structure because they like the idea that they are receiving better terms from the GP and their money isn't sitting idle. Perhaps this would be true if you believe the unlikely assumption that this term doesn't change GP behavior. I strongly dislike this structure because it incentivizes GPs to make investments quickly to match the pace of their fundraising, rather than to wait patiently for the best deals and throttle their fundraising based on market conditions. Even the most disciplined GPs hate to see un-invested cash sitting idle in their account and "burning pref". This, I propose, is not the incentive LPs should want GPs to have. Large funds with ticking clocks are notorious for overpaying for anything and everything to get their money spent. Take the long-term view and give up some preferred return in exchange for better incentives.

Overlap

Having multiple sources of equity capital is a good thing for GPs. Different sources (for instance a pension investor side account, co-mingled fund, syndication business, or potential JV partner) have different real estate appetites and hot buttons, so more sources can mean the potential to do more deals. As long as there isn't too much overlap between equity sources, this is fine. If a deal could fit for more than one source however, the GP faces a potential problem: who should get the deal?

Often the default answer is that GPs do the best deals (or all deals if they have more equity than deals) with the most profitable equity source. Profitable for the GP means having high fees, low preferred returns, high promotes, or other GP-friendly terms. This can end up being good for smaller fund or syndicate investors with "retail" terms (higher fees and promotes). Since they are generally the most profitable equity source, they can end up getting first dibs on deals.

To counteract this incentive, some institutional or large JV investors will negotiate to have a first right of refusal on all deals with a GP. Despite the lower fee/promote structure, this arrangement still may make sense for the GP if the large LP has the capacity to do many deals over a long period of time.

Even GPs with a single fund-based source of equity can run into conflicts of interest. They often operate a series of funds to create a smooth and sustainable business. To avoid downtime between funds, fund investment periods can overlap, meaning the same GP may be able to buy a property with multiple funds and may have some discretion about where to put it. If an older fund isn't performing well, better deals could be cherry picked for a newer fund with the benefit of a fresh start. Or perhaps good deals will be steered to newer funds to make the fundraising process easier.

As the Notorious B.I.G. said, "It's like the more money we come across, the more problems we see." There are too many variations to come up with an overall strategy or rule of thumb. Your best bet is to take the time to understand the manager's business model and use your judgement to decide if you're comfortable with it.

Investor Classes

Nearly every transaction has multiple classes of investors who receive different terms within the same partnership. We mentioned earlier that incentives are offered for early investors to make up for the informational disadvantage they face by committing early to a fund. This is one example of a class or sub-class of investors. The GP's special economic terms are usually accomplished by creating a special class of ownership that receives the promote or fees from a transaction.

GPs can't provide special treatment to some investors over others based purely on whim, but they can create special classes for investors to address legitimate differences between them. The early investors discussed above have a preferred class due to the additional risk they take. The GP has a special class to compensate it for finding and arranging the transaction or fund. Often large investors will have preferred terms, which are only available to those who commit to a minimum investment amount. Exchange investors often participate as a class separate from new investors.

Special classes of investors are not unique to funds, they also are common in syndicated deals, although the longer fundraising timeline and complexities of the structure make them particularly helpful for comingled funds. The various classes of investors will be disclosed in the PPM. Review it and see if you qualify for a class with preferred terms.

Alignment of Interest: The Great Misnomer

The coffee is great. So is the view of the city from the main conference room. High end chairs, an imposing spotless glass conference table, CNBC on mute in the corner... everything looks like business. The deal seems like it makes sense, and the team knows what they are doing. Still, this is a big investment for you and there are real risks. That big tenant is rolling soon and who knows what you will have to spend on tenant improvements to fill that space if they play hardball on rents. Then the partner tells you something that makes you feel better: He is contributing 10% of the equity in the deal. Half of that will be new cash. (That's seven figures, more than ten times what your share will cost.) He tells you how he will be the biggest investor in the deal and has more to lose than anyone, that his interests are highly aligned with partners. You feel better knowing that he will have the same motivation and perspective on the deal as you... but should you?

Well, sort of. The reality is that GP investments are fundamentally different than LPs'. This mismatch means that truly aligned interests are like the Yeti; their existence is possible in theory but never witnessed in practice. While I think the vast majority of deal sponsors take their fiduciary responsibility very seriously and consider their investors' interests carefully when making decisions, this doesn't mean their interests are well aligned. This misconception has caused investors to favor promotes over fees as a method of compensation, and as a result the industry takes more risk than it should.

While the usual mishmash of fees, expense reimbursements, and promotes can seem odious, the combination of different compensation types smooths extreme misalignments of interest and provides managers with revenue that roughly matches company expenses and creates meaningful performance incentives.

The impossibility of aligning interests is something managers don't advertise (for obvious reasons) and investors don't like to admit to themselves. It means investors have to place trust in managers to do the right thing for partners even if they are incentivized to do otherwise. How do you test for this character trait? As discussed previously, track records, big organizations, and persuasive pitches don't measure it well. Investors like to believe that they can quantify investment risks. (Where does this sit on the efficient frontier? What is the correlation to my equity portfolio? What is the standard deviation of five-year returns?) Frustratingly, private real estate investments resist quantification and are inseparable from the people who manage them.

To really understand the magnitude of this issue, let's think about the real estate business from the perspective of the operator. Most operators are capital constrained. As a result, effectively growing a real estate company isn't about profiting from investing house money in good real estate deals. Companies grow by putting enough cash in a deal to demonstrate reasonable skin in the game, then magnifying this investment by earning fees, and creating an option that the promote will pay off. The smaller the initial investment, the more this arrangement can be replicated and the faster the company (and the net worth of the founders) can grow. Because GPs profit disproportionately from deals that outperform, and real estate outcomes are more uncertain than anyone wants to admit, it makes sense to do as many deals (generate as many of these promote call options) as possible.

After wading through an eighty-page PPM, it's easy to lose sight of the bigger picture. When all the partnership terms are considered, how much of an impact do they have on an LP investment and what do they mean to the GP? These economics may not be described as such in the offering materials, but you can be sure any moderately sophisticated GP knows them inside out for every deal they do.

Modeling this structure can be a complicated endeavor, particularly when combined with the inherent complexity of the underlying real estate. For the sake of simplicity, let's separate the compensation structure from the real estate by looking at hypothetical investment returns to GPs and LPs based on a range of property IRRs. For an actual transaction, we would then need to take the further step of forecasting our expected property returns, and of course understanding the range of likely upside and downside scenarios and what they would mean to each party. This isn't something you need to do in practice for each deal, but going through it is a good way to get an intuitive sense of deal economics.

Many investors, perhaps rightly, focus on LP IRRs and the dilution to returns caused by GP load. This has merits, but let's use multiples for the moment because the differences between GP and LP IRRs are big enough to make visual charts impractical. For our purposes, the multiple is the total amount of cash received from an investment divided by the total amount of cash invested; pretty simple, right?

Because there are an infinite number of potential structures, a relatively common structure is chosen for this example:

- $20,000,000 acquisition, financed with a 75% LTV loan, plus $2,000,000 in transaction fees and capex funds.
- Five-year investment horizon
- Fees to GP: 1% acquisition fee, 1% disposition fee
- GP to invest 10% of equity ($200,000 from 1% acquisition fee, $800,000 of new cash)
- 8% preferred return, 80/20 to a 12%, 70/30 to a 15%, 60/40 thereafter

For the sake of simplicity let's assume all cash is distributed at disposition and equity IRRs are net of all operational and transactional expenses (such as selling broker fees or financing fees) except for those paid to the GP.

The X-axis of the following chart shows a range of property level equity IRRs. The Y axis is the multiple on invested equity. The chart shows two lines; one representing the GP's multiple on invested equity ($800,000 of new cash), and one showing the LP's multiple on invested equity (property level returns less GP load).

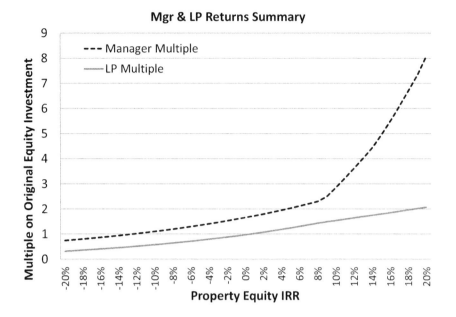

Still with us? Great. Let's talk about what this means, starting with bad outcomes and proceeding to good ones.

First, although we can't see it on this chart, if the deal completely craters, resulting in a 100% loss of equity, everyone loses their entire investment. Clearly, this is a terrible outcome for everyone. The GP has every reason to avoid this whenever possible.

The left half of the chart shows negative returns. Note that LP multiples are all below one in this section and increase steadily as property returns increase. At a zero IRR, LP multiples are still slightly negative (around 0.97) due to fee load. At around ½% IRR the LPs break even. Throughout this section, GP multiples are also poor to unspectacular, but consistently better than LP multiples due to the impact of the acquisition fee and disposition fees. Because they are not performance based (part of the distribution waterfall), they boost GP returns, making up partially for poor investment returns on the GP's cash contribution.

This trend continues until LP IRRs reach the preferred return of 8%, at which point things become much more interesting. The slope of the GP multiple jumps up quickly at this point, the result of the 20% profits interest distribution to the

GP in addition to its pro-rata LP distributions. Although difficult to see with the scale of the chart, LP returns flatten out slightly for the same reason. The impact to LPs is less pronounced than that to the GP because, as discussed previously, the GP co-investment is small enough that even a modest portion of project distributions can significantly impact returns.

Although hard to see with the scale, similar kinks in the multiple curve occur at the subsequent LP IRR hurdles of 12% and 15%.

Take another look at the chart. Would you describe GP interests here as well aligned with LP interests? From the perspective of a GP, the goodness of a good outcome is much more significant than the badness of a bad outcome. That's basically all you need to know to understand the private real estate business.

I first learned this lesson accidently in an 8th grade class designed to teach students about money and investing. As part of the class, our teacher explained the basics of buying stocks and the benefits of owning a diversified portfolio. Our class project was an investment contest where we created and managed a virtual portfolio, then compared results to find out who won. Although the purported lesson of the class was to learn to diversify, there is no good way to measure risk adjusted returns with a project like this, so the winner was crowned based on performance alone. Mind you, this was in the days of daily newspaper stock quotes, before the age of online brokerage accounts. Creating and tracking the value of a complicated portfolio was time consuming and tedious. Most of my peers applied the lessons of the class and created thoughtfully diversified portfolios. I put all the money in a single stock, Boeing as I recall. The rationale, if anything other than simplicity of calculation, for the choice escapes me now. Whatever the reason, it certainly had nothing to do with investing skill. Boeing announced something or other, the stock ticked up, and I won.

Obviously, this win had nothing to do with skill. I rolled the dice and they fell in my favor. Making the riskiest bet possible is your best shot at winning in this type of contest. Likewise, in the world of syndicated real estate investing, GPs earn big promotes from successful deals. Like gambling in a casino where the odds are in your favor, GPs are well advised to place as many bets as possible, maximizing risk and playing the odds. They aren't well compensated for making smart, safe, conservative investments, at least not in the short to medium term. I vividly remember recognizing this unintentional lesson while sweating in my eighth-grade classroom waiting for summer vacation to start, and here I am many years later in real estate. I guess the lesson stuck.

H.L. Mencken once described democracy as "the theory that the common people know what they want and deserve to get it good and hard". The same sentiment might be applied, less than charitably, to describe how competition for LP dollars has created the bizarre set of terms common in private partnerships. To be fair, many investors also dislike the typical structure too... yet on it continues.

Having spent time seated on both sides of the table, I have some sympathy for everyone involved. Incentive and fee structures have emerged naturally over time to address concerns from all parties. As complicated and faulty as the typical deal structure can be, it tends to create acceptable alignments of interest while still maintaining a mechanism for managers to generate cash to pay overhead. Winston Churchill was a bit less cynical than Mencken, calling democracy "the worst form of government, except for all the others". The same might be said for deal structures. This isn't a story about good and bad, it's a story about what is. As long as you understand and accept it, it's the best solution we have.

CHAPTER 5: JOINT VENTURES & EXCHANGE/TIC CONSIDERATIONS

"We shape our dwellings, and afterwards our dwellings shape us." – Sir Winston Churchill

Most of our discussion so far has revolved around syndicated or fund transactions involving many LPs, each investing a small percentage of the total equity capitalization. Let's change our focus for the moment to talk about the special case of larger investors like family offices, endowments and the like. These investors face some unique opportunities and challenges when allocating money to private real estate.

Many investors participate in syndications because they simply don't have enough cash to create a sufficiently diversified portfolio of real estate through direct ownership of properties. True joint venture (JV) investors who can individually capitalize properties have major advantages over syndicate investors. If you're fortunate enough to be in this situation, congratulations, but keep in mind that the benefits involved with JV investing come with an additional set of complications that need to be considered.

First, the structure of JV investments. You may recall from our previous discussion the generalized model of a simple JV investment structure:

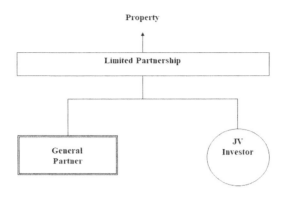

Simple JV Structure

The primary difference between a JV investment and a syndicated investment is the number of LP investors; 1 in the case of a JV, and multiple in the case of a syndicate. This results in changes to a variety of terms in the partnership to reflect the larger investment amount and percentage ownership of JV investors.

GP Co-invest & Compensation

Typical JV LP investors provide 80% to 95% of the equity for a transaction, with the balance being provided by the GP. The amount of co-invest by the GP impacts the terms of the transaction. Usually higher GP co-invests result in more favorable terms to the GP such as lower preferred returns and higher promote splits. Regardless of co-invest amount, JV investor terms are generally more favorable to the LP than they would be in syndicated deals.

Major Decisions & Removal Rights

Because JV investors provide the majority of the equity for the transaction, they get to call the shots... mostly. So called "control provisions" describe who gets to decide what in a partnership. Most JV investors don't want the burden of making day-to-day decisions about property operations, which are mostly left to the GP to handle. Major decisions, however, usually are controlled by or require the approval of the JV partner. Typical major decisions include:
- Buying or selling the property,
- Mortgage financing or refinancing,

- Making a significant investment in the property (new roofs, replacing a major system, etc.),
- Signing a long-term contract with a third party,
- Approval of annual budgets and approval of material variances from it,
- Amendments to the JV agreement,
- Compensation changes to the GP,
- Capital contributions, and
- Approval of insurance terms.

The exact details of what constitutes a major decision are negotiable and vary from deal to deal, but those are common items. In some cases, both the LP and the GP will need to approve certain items. It's also not unusual to have some pre-negotiated limitations on LP control, such as a required hold period before selling a property.

In addition to major decisions relating to the property, JV investors often have some ability to remove the GP from the transaction if they are displeased about the performance of the GP or the investment. What, exactly, constitutes grounds for removal is a negotiated point, as is the impact this could have on the GP's fees, promote, and investment in the transaction. GPs are understandably sensitive about this provision and want to ensure they can only be kicked out for good reason and will be reasonably compensated for their time and effort if it happens.

Financing & Recourse

Borrower strength is a key factor for lenders as they evaluate the potential risk involved in making a loan. The concept of strength includes both financial wherewithal (net worth and liquidity mostly) as well as investment and operating experience. Stronger borrowers are lower risk from a credit perspective, so they get better loan terms. In nearly all transactions, the GP acts as a key principal and guarantor for the lender. Lenders rely on the key principal as the real estate expert and require them to remain responsible for day-to-day operations. Changing a key principal requires lender review and approval of the new replacement key principal. For recourse deals, being a guarantor means providing a personal or corporate guarantee to the lender for some or all of the loan amount, required interest payments, or completion of planned construction or improvements to the property. For non-recourse deals, the GP still takes on carve-out recourse for "bad boy" items such as fraud, misrepresentation, and waste.

For syndicates with fragmented ownership among many LPs, the GP is the only key principal and guarantor required because each LP has limited control over important decisions. For JV transactions however, the lender recognizes that the JV investor retains control over major decisions about property operations and could potentially make decisions that put the lender's collateral (the property) at risk. As a result, lenders often require both the GP and JV investor to be fully underwritten and approved as a borrower during the loan application process. Often the GP remains the only key principal on the loan, but the JV investor may be pre-approved to become a key principal if the GP is removed from the partnership. Likewise, the JV investor may take on some or all of the recourse for the loan if the GP is unable to or the LP can simply obtain better terms. Lenders are understandably careful to consider so called "change in control provisions" in partnership documents, to ensure they know what events might result in the LP becoming the new GP.

Buy/Sell

While JV partners end up with the right to make or approve most major decisions, the timing of the sale of a property can be the subject of much negotiation. Most of the disagreements I hear about between JV partners involve disposition timing. Given the long-term nature of real estate deals, it's extremely common for one party to want to liquidate a deal while the other wants to hold. It could simply be a disagreement about the potential for future growth in a market, a disagreement about the need to invest additional capital in a property, or one party could have a need for liquidity that is totally unrelated to the real estate.

One important and commonly used tool to help address this problem is the inclusion of a buy-sell provision in the partnership agreement. A buy-sell is a mechanism that can be triggered by one or either party if there is a disagreement about whether to hold a property. When I was a kid, and there was desert to be split, my dad would have me cut the desert in half, then he would choose which half he wanted. I became very precise about the symmetry of my pie slices. This is pretty much how a buy-sell works with real estate. One party picks a price, and the other party decides whether they want to buy out their partner or sell their share of the property at that price. This keeps either part from feeling like they are being exploited or being forced to transact at an unfair value.

Even though this issue can seem unlikely when you're buying a property, make sure it's included in your agreement – you could be very happy about it later.

Timing & Process

There are a variety of other unique terms involved in JV deals, such as deposit sharing arrangements and reporting obligations. Although the overall structure of a JV can be simpler in some respects than a syndicate or fund offering, each agreement is bespoke and engaging expert legal counsel and accountants is critical to ensure the ultimate agreement and legal structure is fair and beneficial to everyone involved. To minimize confusion and mistakes, it helps to put together a detailed term sheet summarizing the overall business agreement. Regardless, investors should plan to spend significant money preparing JV deals – money that will be spent whether the deal closes or not.

This additional paperwork takes a lot of time, particularly on your first transaction with a new GP or lender. As a result, JV investors need to be involved in transactions much earlier than syndicate investors. While syndicate investors often see an offering after the bulk of the due diligence process and loan processing has taken place, JV investors work with GPs long before offers are submitted to define what deals are acceptable, convince the seller that the JV investor is committed to buy the deal, and to allow time for the JV agreement and the lender underwriting to be finalized during the due diligence process. Although the structure can have significant benefits for the investor, JV investing is time consuming, and investors often need to chase multiple deals before finding one that works.

Major Investors

Some investors are neither typical passive syndicate LPs nor true JV investors, for instance an investor providing $5M of the equity in a deal requiring $15M. I'll refer to someone like this as a major investor. Major investors are in a tricky middle ground; because they aren't the only equity in the deal and they can't negotiate their own terms, they may need to live with offering terms provided to other smaller syndicate investors. Although sometimes they can be given more favorable economic terms, this is a tricky area where there are some limitations on GPs flexibility due to offering regulations. Because they don't represent a majority of the equity, they don't usually have the voting power needed to control major decisions, so can be subject to the whims of the GP (who may have a fraction of their economic interest in the deal). Adding to the pain, many lenders require investors who hold more than 20% to 25% of the equity interests in a deal (or control a TIC entity) to go through the same rigorous financial underwriting as the GP.

Despite some of these downsides, it sometimes makes sense to be a major investor. I see this situation most often when a 1031 exchange is involved. Many exchange investors want to defer as much of their tax burden as possible (which means they want to re-invest most if not all of their sale proceeds, often enough to qualify as a major investor) but are reluctant to take on more risk by adding significant new cash to a deal (which might be necessary to become a JV investor unless the deal sizes work out very well). As mentioned elsewhere in this book, taking advantage of 1031 exchanges can have significant benefits but also involve significant complexity. Among other things, exchange investors need to contribute their capital in a TIC structure, requiring additional organizational complexity for the entire transaction and another layer of agreements relating to the management of the real estate and the interaction of the various TIC entities. As an exchange investor, you may also either face a partial tax bill or need to add new cash to a transaction to cover your share of capital expenses (which are not an allowable use of exchange proceeds) or to avoid mortgage boot (depending on the capital structures of your upleg and downleg properties). Long story short, if you plan to invest exchange money in a deal, expect to pay plenty of fees, go through lots of brain damage, and live with little to no practical control over the replacement property. As you consider your tax bill, take these factors into account when you decide whether to exchange. Remember also, that taxes will eventually be due and you don't want to exchange into a bad deal that will leave you with a loss of your equity combined with a huge tax liability from previous deals.

From an operator perspective, there are benefits and drawbacks of working with either JV or major investors. Because these investors are larger, there are fewer outside groups to work with. This can simplify the equity raising process, but it can also create risk if a large investor backs out of a deal late in the process. It's normal to have some drop-outs in a syndicated deal with 30-40 investors, but having a large investor bail late in the deal process can sink the deal if it's too late to find the missing equity, and result in significant costs to the GP from due diligence/third party expenses, lender deposits, or deal deposits.

Doing JV or major investor transactions requires a well-orchestrated process between investor and manager, along with a relationship based on clear communication and mutual trust. Being honest and clear about your level of interest is particularly important for large investments. If a deal doesn't suit you, say so. Managers much prefer a "quick no" to a time consuming and ultimately fruitless broken deal. As you negotiate agreements, don't get bogged down in little details. Take the long view – a true partnership ideally will last for many transactions. Don't accept an unreasonable deal, but make sure you are being at least long-term greedy.

CHAPTER 6: MODELING, VALUATIONS, & RETURN PROJECTIONS

"In preparing for battle I have always found that plans are useless, but planning is indispensable." Dwight D. Eisenhower

As someone who began his career as an engineer and spent much of the rest of it in one area of finance or another, more hours than I care to admit have been spent bathed in the cold glow of spreadsheets. I readily admit to being obsessive about models. It is not enough for them to simply obtain the right answer. They need to be elegantly constructed, minimize unnecessary or redundant calculations, and be aesthetically pleasing and comprehensible to people who didn't build them. I can hear my colleagues' eyes roll as I regale them with my opinions on the number of significant digits shown, inconsistent borders, brittle coding, or a plethora of other misdemeanors. I'm unable to help myself. A good model is a thing of beauty; worth creating for its own sake. Building quality models is a sign that you have respect for your craft and take your work seriously. This is how I was taught and at this point in my career, my opinions on modeling are lodged deeply, inextricably within me.

I bring up my fussy tendencies not to lecture you about modeling, but so you can appreciate how hard it is for me to admit that most modeling serves less to unearth truth than as a marketing tool, justifying past decisions to investors and making recommendations and projections appear more precise and considered than they truly are. Like it or not though, financial models are unavoidable. They are a basic tool for real estate professionals. The carpenter's tape measure, the painter's brush, and the cowboy's horse.

Although many investors never perform their own valuations, understanding the modeling and valuation process is critical to being able to evaluate investment offerings. This understanding allows you to follow the logic of the investment thesis and understand the critical assumptions driving investment return and potential risk. Although most people believe that modeling real estate is about determining The Property Value, it's really an exercise in understanding the texture of your investment. Thinking through assumptions, uncertainties, mechanics, and sensitivities provides an intuitive understanding of a deal in a different but equally valuable way as walking a property and peering through the windows. This chapter provides an overview to the valuation and modeling process, hopefully enough that you can better evaluate offerings and call B.S. when you see it.

There are three basic ways to decide what a property is worth. Reviewing comparable sales, calculating replacement cost, and running a discounted cash flow model. Each has its nuances, benefits, and drawbacks. The first two are the simplest so let's blow through those before bogging down on the last.

Comparable Sales

If you're buying or selling a publicly traded liquid security, knowing its price in the market is easy. Let's consider a REIT stock like Equity Residential (EQR). Other people are buying and selling the exact same thing constantly, so you can pull up your handy browser or call your friendly broker and know within seconds precisely how much others are paying for a share of EQR.

Looking at comparable transactions ("comps") lets us value real estate using the same thought process – deciding what you think a property is worth by looking at what other people are paying for similar properties. Part of the difficulty (fun?) of real estate is that no two properties are identical. Even similar properties have different locations, nuances to construction, perhaps different management companies using different leasing approaches. Setting aside the properties, transactions can be skewed by buyer or seller circumstances and negotiations too. Perhaps the buyer was running out of time to place a 1031 exchange and was willing to overpay for a property to avoid taxes. Maybe a bank was selling a property, wanted it off their books before their fiscal year end, and was willing to take a loss to get the deal done. Possibly the deal was being sold with unattractive debt that had to be assumed by the buyer. The possibilities are endless.

Since this is the real world, we just look at the data points we have and do our best. To review comps, the most recent transactions that have a similar profile to the deal being reviewed are pulled from a database. There are a variety of databases, mostly relatively expensive subscription services like Costar that provide additional information beyond just the date and price of each transaction. Comps are narrowed down based on the date of the sale (more recent is better), the location, the price, buyer and seller, property age, size, and other general information. Based on these sales, a value can be triangulated by considering these differences and deciding what they imply about the value of the subject property. This is much more an art than a science.

This process is particularly useful for specialist operators who are underwriting and offering on essentially every deal in their market. Having detailed underwriting completed for each of the comps, having toured each property previously, and usually knowing the back story on both the buyer and the seller of the deals, changes the comps process from a rough estimate into a rich tapestry of history about the marketplace of buyers and sellers.

Like a stock ticker, comps can only tell you what other people are paying for other properties. This has real value though - if everyone else is overlooking a market opportunity, there is no reason to pay more for properties than you need to! Just keep in mind that relying on comps doesn't prevent you from being stupid, it just prevents you from being stupider than all the other active buyers. What we really care about is making good investment decisions, so comps are only part of the puzzle.

Replacement Cost

Replacement cost analysis, or the cost approach to valuation, is similar in concept to comparable analysis. The process is simple. First, figure out how much it would cost to replace the property, accounting for land value, soft costs (entitlement, legal, and design), and hard construction costs. If your cost basis in the subject property (purchase price, capex, and closing costs) is higher than replacement cost, a developer could profitably build new competitive property. The bigger the premium, the larger the profit and the higher the probability development will happen. 20%-25% is a reasonable profit margin to justify taking on the risk of development, but this can vary widely depending on circumstances. Some replacement cost calculations include required developer profit, some do not. So called "Insurable Value" analysis generally just includes the expected cost of sticks and bricks - leaving out soft costs and developer profit under the assumption that the cost to rebuild an existing property would not include those items. Usually replacement cost is communicated in terms of cost, cost per square foot, and/or cost per unit, which allows us to generalize the results across similar properties of different size.

Developers will continue to build as long as it is profitable, driving down rents and values for existing properties until they fall back in line with replacement cost. Although the math looks precise on paper, input costs and market conditions move fast, so replacement cost is a noisy and uncertain metric. Think about this less as a bright red line and more like a fuzzy range. Many a developer's fortune has been made or lost on the margins of these assumptions. Our goal here is not to precisely value the real estate as much as to determine a ceiling on value. As investors, the more we are paying above this ceiling, the more we are exposed to development risk.

The beauty of replacement cost analysis is its simplicity, but like many simple metrics, it has a few shortcomings. The first is defining replacement cost, which is more difficult than one might imagine. The process works by adding up the components of value, each of which has its own nuances:

Land value: Before you can build something, you need somewhere to build it. Land is the most basic, and often the most volatile, component that goes into a development. Sales comp analysis is used to determine how much developers are paying for similar parcels of land in the area. Each comp needs to be examined to adjust for the planned use (sites zoned for different uses are often not helpful), the state of entitlements (is it ready to build or is significant money needed to obtain approvals for construction), allowed density, quality of the location, and other factors. Although it is sometimes described in terms of raw cost per acre or square foot, land value is commonly communicated in terms of its contribution to the cost of the planned final product. In other words, we calculate how many dollars per square foot of office building or per unit of apartments the underlying land costs. As an example, if a site allows 100 apartments and costs $5,000,000, the land is worth $50,000 per unit. Thinking about land value this way helps correct for some of the differences in entitlements and densities that exist between sites.

The most common problem with valuing land is coming up with enough similar comps to be able to accurately value a site. In most cities, if there are enough good comps to accurately nail down your land value, you are already facing an impending development problem. If there aren't great comps, valuing the land is tough.

In practice, land value is calculated by developers in reverse; it is the residual value left over after subtracting all other costs and profit from the projected final property value. Unfortunately, this backward analysis, while useful for valuing land, is not helpful for us as we build up the replacement cost for an existing property. Like property sales comps, land comp analysis tells us how much land trades for today but doesn't tell us what it should inherently be worth or how that value has changed over time. Because land value is determined by development profitability, it is notoriously volatile; swinging between all-time highs in economic booms and effectively zero (or negative if it requires carrying costs) in recessions.

Investing in land is a complex discipline and specialty in itself, and beyond the scope of this book. I bring this up only to say that coming up with land value is at best a temporal and uncertain process, and at worst it's a complete wild ass guess. Keep that in mind as you think about the value of replacement cost analysis.

Soft costs: This portion of the value stack includes the costs of entitlement, architecture, legal, and other non-construction costs. It is notoriously difficult to estimate, partially because these costs can vary widely based on the strategy of each developer. Cutting edge projects that blaze new trails in design and site use may command a premium (or discount if they're badly executed) when they are complete, but they can rack up significant design costs along the way and need to overcome entitlement hurdles. On the other hand, cookie-cutter developers pumping out the next in a long series of identical developments can re-use elements of prior deals, making their projects significantly more cost effective, if not particularly interesting. Each site has its own unique development hurdles to overcome, further complicating the process of estimating soft costs. Lastly, states and cities vary widely in their policy toward development. Developments are encouraged in some areas through tax or other incentives and are guaranteed to be a long and prolonged battle in others. Given all this uncertainty, how are soft costs estimated? Unfortunately, there is no great way to estimate them. Most groups use a rule of thumb based on local norms and recent transactions.

Hard costs: Often a third-party provider like Marshall & Swift is used to add up the current cost of reconstructing the subject property. These services have good access to current costs and are relatively accurate in their estimates based on a snapshot of current prices, at least in comparison to our imprecise estimates of land and soft costs. Still, prices for lumber, steel, labor, and other contributions to cost can change rapidly, quickly making these estimates obsolete.

Adding these components together gives us our best estimate for replacement cost and is usually what you will see in an appraisal or an offering memorandum. Setting aside the uncertainties of each contribution of cost, we face a more difficult problem for older properties; the underlying assumption of like-kind replacement. Because of changing regulations and design features over time, older properties are often built in a way that could not or would not be replicated if a developer were to design and build a competitive property from scratch today. Take for example an old single-story low-density apartment property surrounded by mid-rise product in an infill submarket. Residents may love the low-density feel of the property (and may pay a significant premium for it), but it would likely not make economic sense for the property to be rebuilt with the same density if a builder were to start from scratch. As a result, new product will be significantly different than the subject property. This could impact values either way. An older property without washer/dryers, dishwashers, and central heating and air conditioning might be cheap to rebuild, but changes in renter preferences might mean that all new properties will include these features and therefore be fundamentally different when they are completed.

This last issue is perhaps the biggest problem with replacement cost analysis and there is no great way to deal with it in practice. Rather than estimate replacement cost for these properties, the better approach is to set aside the specifics of the subject property and simply decide if new competitive development is profitable in the current market. If you are thinking about purchasing an office building and no new office buildings are in development because rents are too low to justify development, that's a good fact. On the other hand, if the development pipeline is full of new office buildings, you can expect persistent downward pressure on office rents. Older buildings will benefit from or be hurt by new development more or less than newer properties depending on their attributes, but at some point the impact of new developments inevitably starts to impact rents at existing properties.

While it's far from a perfect science, it's good investment practice to think about replacement cost while keeping in mind it's imprecision and shortfalls. Like comparable analysis, it is one more tool preventing us from being unnecessarily stupid. For those of us eschewing fix-and-flip strategies for long-term real estate allocation, knowing where you are in the development cycle is critical to long-term investment success and discount to replacement cost is a good leading indicator of your current position in the long term real estate cycle.

Discounted Cash Flow (DCF) or Income Capitalization Approach

Let us now set aside the imprecise and flawed comparable sale and replacement cost methods and behold the holy grail of real estate valuation: the discounted cash flow (DCF) model. As you no doubt know, real estate investment is all about cash flow. We spend cash to buy and improve properties, and in return expect a large enough stream of cash to be generated from those properties to justify our investment. Cash flow models are elegant constructs that estimate the sources and uses of cash (as well as the timing and risk of each) over the life of an investment, allowing us to back into the implied value of the property.

A detailed look at DCF modeling is beyond the scope of this book, but knowing a few concepts will give you great insights into the practice of real estate valuation and the operation of investment companies. For better or worse, we are in the epoch of the financial analysts. DCFs are the basis for nearly all investment valuation in real estate as well as in the corporate world. Excel has revolutionized the real estate acquisitions process. Let's delve briefly into the sausage making process. It's a bit tedious and not very pretty, but you might as well know the truth about your meal given how much it costs!

Modeling deviates a bit between classroom and boardroom, at least in my experience. In the classroom, DCF models are created as follows:

1. Forecast cash flows going into and out of a project (purchase price, operating distributions, sale proceeds, etc.),
2. Assign a date to each cash flow,
3. Assign a discount rate to each type of cash flow,
4. Discount each cash flow to current value,
5. Add up all the discounted cash flows; this is the net present value ("NPV"). If they sum to a positive number you should do the deal, and if they sum to a negative number you shouldn't.

This is more or less what everyone learns in school. In the real world, the process is reversed and looks like this:

1. Forecast cash flows going into and out of a project (purchase price, operating distributions, sale proceeds, etc.),
2. Assign a date to each cash flow,
3. Figure out what discount rate makes the NPV equal zero. This rate is the investment's projected internal rate of return ("IRR").
4. Investors evaluate the IRR to decide if the projected return is high enough to justify the risk, and specialist operators can compare the IRR to other similar transactions to decide if it provides a better or worse risk adjusted return in comparison to other comparable deals.

This second process, the one most commonly used by practitioners, makes it a bit easier to compare different transactions of different sizes and provides slightly more intuitive outputs. Excel's XIRR function (or similar calculations performed by other software) makes this otherwise unwieldy calculation easy and quick. There are some technical reasons why and very few unusual circumstances when it could be problematic (which finance professors will be quick to point out) but none of these are common in practice and they can be easily flagged and dealt with by experienced modelers on all but the most complex transactions.

Investors use their experience as a guide to decide what IRR is appropriate for each deal. Even within asset classes, required IRRs should fluctuate based on deal specifics like leverage levels, execution risk, asset quality, and uncertainty of assumptions. When a deal is being evaluated, the model is set up, and the investor simply decides how high the purchase price can go before the projected IRR is unacceptably low. Voila – now we know the highest price we should be willing to pay for a property.

Easy, right? The basic theory is straightforward. Even if you have better things to do with your time than build models, at least you now understand how they work.

While the theory is simple, models themselves are highly complex. Most full models include a series of sub-models that forecast the important factors impacting the investment: debt terms and an associated payment schedule (along with interest rate forecasts for floating rate debt), upfront capital budgets, recurring capital budgets, revenue forecasts, operating budgets and forecasts, market forecasts, and exit projections. Robust models also layer scenario analysis on top of each assumption to help examine the impact of better or worse than expected outcomes on the investment.

Even for practitioners, going through another company's model can be a confusing and frustrating experience. The reality of modeling is that even relatively simple investments in real life are extremely complicated to replicate in Excel. Why do I bring this up? There is nothing inherently wrong with cash flow modeling, but the complexity of financial modeling makes it rife with opportunities for both unintentional mistakes and outright purposeful misuse.

A side note about Argus: Many commercial firms use a specialized modeling software called Argus which is essentially a cash flow model customized for real estate investments. Argus can be helpful because it simplifies the input of modeling assumptions (Argus runs can easily be exported and shared between users) making it faster and easier to underwrite properties. Its standardization also helps avoid simple calculation errors that are the bane and fear of Excel users. The downside of Argus is its limited flexibility to handle unique situations, which are common in real estate deals. I tend to focus more on Excel models, not because I have anything against Argus, but because it's rarely used in the multifamily industry.

Even small assumptions can have a material impact on return projections, and no assumption is too small to be considered. Should "other income" grow at market rent growth rates or at the rate of inflation? How much will the implementation of a utility reimbursement program impact net rental rates? How should buying an additional two years of prepayment flexibility on a ten-year loan impact the projected exit cap rate? No minutiae are too small to be overlooked. In most cases, investors have neither the access to models nor the expertise necessary to really evaluate investment forecasts. From the outside, it is difficult to objectively determine if an operator is being aggressive or conservative with their projections.

There is no easy way to fix this problem, other than to do your best to pick quality operators based on the other evaluation metrics described in this book. Notwithstanding the foregoing, there are a few assumptions worth looking at for every deal. These assumptions have the biggest impact on valuation:

- Current market lease rates
- Rent growth over the projected hold period
- Expense budget (in comparison to seller's actual)
- Interest rate forecasts
- Exit cap rate

After all the ingredients are put in the black box, out comes the result: the projected investment IRR. The beauty of the IRR is its simplicity; it can easily be used to compare otherwise very different investments. This simplicity, and its universality, is also a curse. This is the first and sometimes only number many investors focus on. They quickly compare it to other deals and often just pick the deal with the highest projected returns. IRRs are easy to compare, risk is not. Both are driven by the realism of the modeling assumptions, which are rarely obvious.

This unfortunate reality leads to bad incentives in the industry. Having a policy of making conservative assumptions puts operators at a disadvantage to their less conservative peers. Investors notice lower projected returns, but not the underlying assumptions.

While complexity and opacity are important problems, they are overwhelmed by the problem of uncertainty. Each of the many assumptions and inputs in a model are estimates of an uncertain future. Some of the inputs to models are very important and have very large amounts of uncertainty. We deal with some of these issues separately in the chapter about market forecasts. In practice, models usually use the most likely (analyst or industry consensus) outcome as the input for each assumption. This combination of inputs creates the base case for the pro forma. If you read through the offering documents and see THE IRR, this is usually where it comes from. The probability of hitting this exact return is of course miniscule in reality given the incredible uncertainties involved.

There are a few ways to deal with this problem. My personal favorite is admittedly a bit of a hack: scenario analysis. In addition to the baseline model so often used to make decisions, run a series of upside and, most importantly, downside scenarios. I like to run multiple versions of the downside scenario between bad and Armageddon. Understanding a deal's ability to withstand bad times is critical. The phrase "protect the downside and the upside will take care of itself" (which, hilariously, is in Donald Trump's "The Art of the Deal") sums up this philosophy. Although this scenario analysis is commonly performed by operators, it is infrequently included in marketing materials. It's a difficult concept to communicate and, let's be honest here, it doesn't sell well. Investors don't like thinking about bad times. Plus, how bad should a downside scenario be? There is no standard or norm for this type of analysis. Thus, the baseline scenario is usually what investors see in offering materials and you will be left to guess about the infinite variety of alternate investment outcomes.

A geekier way of modeling uncertainty is a souped-up version of scenario analysis: Monte Carlo simulations. Each assumption's input, rather than being a single number, is made as a probability distribution of numbers. So as an example, rent growth could be input as a normal distribution with an average of 3% and a standard deviation of 2%. Each input has separate assumptions, even correlations between inputs, such as: if interest rates are higher, so are cap rates. Then the computer runs thousands or millions of random scenarios and shows you the expected distribution of outcomes. The engineer in me loves these tools because they are simply awesome. Unfortunately, assigning distributions and correlations to inputs is tough to do with any precision, so the results look more precise than they should. Also, it's hard enough to clearly communicate a simple return model, let alone a monstrosity like a Monte Carlo simulation.

My advice is to not take the projected IRR too seriously. Experienced real estate practitioners and financial engineers can easily bend it to their whim. Internally, financial models are an excellent tool for operators, allowing them to better understand, evaluate, and negotiate deals. In most investment offerings though, models act more as a marketing tool than a scientific one; they serve to show investors that an operator is asking sophisticated looking questions on their behalf, but not much more. Total modeling luddites miss out on a valuable tool, but investors are well served by maintaining a healthy dose of skepticism.

The process of calculating IRRs is reminiscent of the search for the answer to the Great Question of Life, the Universe, and Everything in Douglas Adams' "The Hitchhiker's Guide to the Galaxy". A supercomputer, Deep Thought, is designed to answer this question precisely. After seven and a half million years of calculations, it returns the answer to this eternal human riddle: Forty-two. Like Deep Thought, our models have no problem spitting out precise answers. Unfortunately, we are rarely capable of, or willing to, ask them the right questions.

CHAPTER 7: METRICS, RATIOS, & QUANTITATIVE MISCELLANY

"The curious task of economics is to demonstrate to men how little they really know about what they imagine they can design." – Friedrich Hayek

The IRR is a critical, if not the most important metric for investors to use when evaluating transactions. Unfortunately, IRRs are slippery and unruly. This is particularly true for highly leveraged deals, which are quite volatile depending on assumptions. Unfortunately, because the practical calculation of IRRs has so many shortcomings, they shouldn't be relied upon as the only metric to consider. Thankfully, there are a variety of other tools available for investors to help evaluate potential real estate investments. Ideally, as many as possible should be considered. These metrics can act as red flags, showing areas of potential risk or concern, or allow other types of understanding beyond a simple projection of return.

Multiples

Investment multiples are perhaps the simplest metric used to define performance. To calculate the multiple, add up all the cash you receive from an investment and divide it by the amount of cash you invested. Cash is cash, whether it comes from operating distributions, refinances, or a disposition. Simple. So simple that it's hard to game, which is one reason why it's sometimes added to the incentive hurdles for investment managers to complement IRR hurdles.

$$Investment\ Multiple = \frac{\text{Cash Received}}{\text{Cash Invested}}$$

The downside of the multiple metric is that it doesn't take into account the hold period. Doubling your money is a lot more impressive over a two-year hold than over a twenty-year hold. For non-compounded returns, adding the element of time allows us to simply translate between multiple and annual return. The chart below shows the relationship between these metrics.

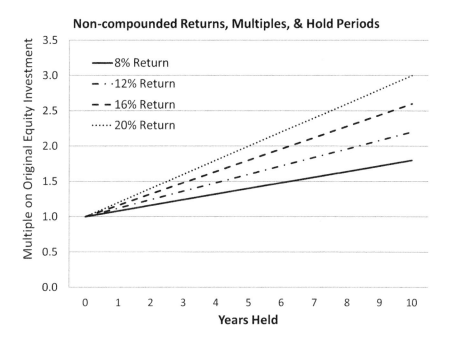

Translating to compounded returns (IRRs) adds another level of complexity due to the impact of the timing of cash flows on the calculation of IRRs. For the sake of illustration, if we assume a simple investment where cash goes in, nothing happens for a period of years, then a single block of cash is returned (imagine a real estate investment with no cash flow distributions... like land), the relationship would look like the following:

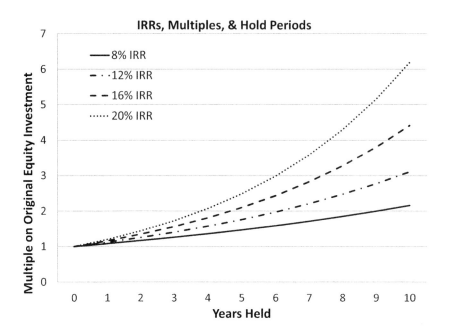

Those of you staving off sleep will note the curvy nature of the lines in comparison to the straight lines of the non-compounded chart, as well as the fact that the actual multiples are much larger for the compounded chart. This illustrates the powerful impact of compounding interest, something you are no doubt aware of if you've ever been subjected to a presentation by a 401k administrator.

Cap Rates

Cap rates are the most common metric used to describe real estate valuations, and for good reason. Investments are about the capacity to generate and distribute cash, so what metric could be more relevant than the cap rate, which is defined as the net operating income ("NOI" – a proxy for cash flow) divided by the purchase price? For corporate investments, the ubiquitous PE ratio is held in equally high esteem.

$$Cap\ Rate\ (\%) = \frac{\text{Net Operating Income (NOI)}}{\text{Purchase Price}}\ X\ 100$$

Indeed, when calculated consistently, cap rates are an indispensable tool for investment professionals to triangulate value as they track a sequence of investments, ensuring that each evaluated deal compares logically to the others under review. For very similar deals, the cap rate should be very similar. For value-add deals cap rates are lower than for an otherwise identical stabilized deal because the property offers the potential for increased NOI. Think of this as the analog to growth stocks trading at high PE ratios, reflecting their potential for increased earnings.

So, what's the problem with cap rates? The issue with cap rates in practice is the caveat mentioned above that cap rates are calculated on a consistent basis. There are countless ways to massage and bully cap rates into telling a desired story, and even well-meaning companies may by convention have different methods of calculating and communicating cap rates, making it difficult for outside investors to compare offerings from different firms.

Although purchase price is most commonly used as the denominator in your cap rate calculation, it can also be helpful to look at the "cost basis" cap rate, including the purchase price, transaction costs, and one-time capital expenditures. The full capitalization is being invested, so you might as well understand your yield on the actual basis in the property.

In the numerator, variations on the NOI calculation are helpful to understand where the property is and where it is headed. Historical cap rates use the seller's actual historical financials, describing the current state of the property. While trailing three month or current rent-roll revenue are sometimes used, it is better to look at the 12-month trailing expenses with any appropriate adjustments to avoid distortions from seasonality or infrequent expenses. Pro forma cap rates adjust operations to reflect changes expected post-closing. New owners may make changes to staffing or marketing, and taxes may be reset to reflect the purchase price; changes that should be considered by investors. Even without changes to revenue, changes to the expense side of the equation can impact NOI significantly. NOIs may be calculated with either the broker's "market standard" (aka "what everyone pretends is reasonable even though it isn't") levels of recurring capex or actual forecast numbers. The former is helpful to normalize the metric when discussing it with other industry players or comparing to other offerings, the latter is more useful as a measure of reality. As-stabilized or asrenovated cap rates adjust revenue for the expected increases generated by the planned investment strategy and may or may not include underwritten increases (or decreases... in theory) due to market forces.

When underwriting deals, I use a matrix of cap rates with variations on price to understand the valuation. Each variation tells a slightly different story about the property's current state and potential. Comparing types of cap rates for the same property is informative too. As an example, the spread between the actual purchase price cap rate and the as-stabilized cost cap rate is a good metric for how much value is being added to a property due to renovation or operational changes. The common question "What was the cap rate on that deal you just closed?" often turns into a longer and more nuanced conversation than you might expect. Much of the value in this exercise comes from the comparison to other historical deals, and the information to do it might not be accessible for an outside investor. Unfortunately, that means some of the most useful aspects of this metric don't help when investors are evaluating offerings.

Should you look at the cap rate and consider it as an important factor? Definitely. As always though, keep in mind the complexities described above. It's just one metric of many, and it can be strongly influenced by underwriting standards and strategy.

Cash on Cash Returns

The cash on cash return is a simple metric used to describe the cash generation potential of an investment. It is calculated by dividing the annual cash generated by an investment by the total cash investment.

$$Cash\ on\ Cash\ Return\ (\%) = \frac{\text{Annual Distributable Cash}}{\text{Total Cash Investment}}\ X\ 100$$

Income focused investors gravitate to this metric because it clearly measures "bang for the buck" in terms of income generation for a given investment. This return makes comparisons to other investment products, like bonds, easier. Ultimately, investment is about the ability to generate cash flow, so this is a reasonable way to think about returns. Unfortunately, cash on cash returns are highly sensitive to other factors, such as the amount of debt used and the term of interest-only payments, making them particularly susceptible to the use of financial engineering. Be careful that you aren't taking on too much risk in search of a marginally higher cash on cash return. Focus on underlying real estate fundamentals and think about whether strong returns are being generated from healthy underlying real estate or risky financial engineering. Over time, good real estate will provide income if it's bought at the right price and managed well.

Current Return

A close relative of the cash on cash return, the current return includes both cash distributions and principal repayment from mortgage amortization. By adding amortization, this metric eliminates the distortion created by interest-only periods.

$$Current\ Return\ (\%) = \frac{Annual\ Distributable\ Cash + Annual\ Amortization}{Total\ Cash\ Investment}\ X\ 100$$

I like this metric better than cash on cash for this reason, but keep in mind that it is still impacted by the terms of the debt. Looking at the current return is a practical way to compare the cash generation potential of a property in relation to its price (cap rate), with an adjustment for the impact of the debt available. After all, most syndicated transactions use debt, so to ignore the impact and cost of the leverage is to ignore a crucial part of the economics of a deal.

Risk Metrics

Because few investors are willing to admit how much uncertainty hides in their assumptions, measuring risk in real estate is tough. While it's hard to quantify, there are some good risk metrics that act as rules of thumb, mostly related to debt underwriting. This is no accident since lenders are primarily concerned with downside risk, whereas equity investors tend to focus more on upside opportunity.

Revenue Stress Test

Although not widely used, my favorite metric to measure risk, the revenue stress test, is simple. The point of this test is to determine how much revenue would need to decline before a property hits cash flow breakeven. Going below breakeven is bad, obviously, so higher stress test numbers are better. To calculate, divide total distributable cash (total revenue less all expenses including debt payments and actual capex) by total revenue. A result of 10% tells you that revenue can decline by 10% before the property becomes distressed.

$$Revenue\ Stress\ Test\ (\%) = \frac{\text{Distributable Cash}}{\text{Total Revenue}} X\ 100$$

When calculating this metric, consider whether it is appropriate to use interest-only payments, amortizing payments, or a stressed payment based on higher rates (appropriate if floating rate debt is being used). I like to use amortizing payments for conservatism on fixed-rate debt, although if a loan is full-term interest-only, it makes more sense to use the IO payments to understand actual holding period risk. For floating rate debt, it may be helpful to create a table or chart calculating the stress test under different interest rate scenarios or to use a "stressed rate", as lenders do, to understand the potential impact of increases in interest rates.

The stress test is similar to the debt coverage ratio ("DCR") test commonly used by lenders, but I prefer it because it provides more useful feedback. As you can see from the chart below run with typical transaction metrics, the two measures are related but not identical. Both tell the same general story; risk decreases as you use less debt.

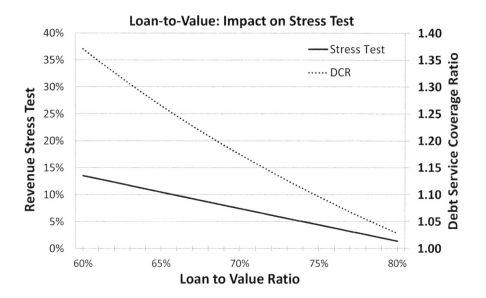

The DCR's shortcoming is that it doesn't provide a very intuitive measurement, whereas the stress test does. Most expenses tend to be fixed, with the notable exception of management fees, which means properties with different expense ratios have varying abilities to tolerate rental declines; something hard to gauge with the DCR. The stress test takes this into account allowing us to focus on the core question: how much volatility can a specific deal tolerate? This allows us to examine historical market rent changes, tenant rollover risk, employer concentration, or other factors and gauge the level of risk in a deal.

Keep in mind that market volatility is normal and expected. As investors, we should be braced for distributions to go up and down periodically. In fact, this uncertainty is one reason why real estate produces returns as attractive as it has historically. But as soon as a property can't meet its cash flow obligations, volatility becomes catastrophic. Unless the partnership recapitalizes, has reserves, or you are blessed with a particularly forgiving lender, the deal is on track to become a 100% loss. Most private partnerships are path dependent – a recovery in property values does you no good if you have already given the property back to the lender. Real estate requires staying power; a trait that private partnerships often lack due to their design and structure.

Loan-to-value (LTV)

Probably the simplest and most important ratio in real estate is the loan-to-value ratio. As simple as it sounds, there are a few ways to calculate it, making it more confusing than it probably should be. The general idea here is to understand how much equity cushion a deal has.

$$Loan\ to\ Value\ (LTV, \%) = \frac{\text{Loan Amount}}{\text{Property Value}} X\ 100$$

"Loan", the numerator, is usually the maximum loan balance approved to be funded by the lender. The trick here is that loans aren't always fully funded at closing. For value add or development loans, the loan funds to an initial level, then supplemental "draws" are funded when additional equity is contributed or pre-defined operational or development hurdles have been successfully completed. Stabilized properties have less uncertainty about the potential loan amount, although many lenders allow for supplemental loans. Typically, the loan balance in these cases is the loan balance funded at closing unless a clear plan is in place in advance to refinance the property as part of the business plan.

"Value", the denominator, has as much or more variety in definition. Most people think of this as the purchase price, and that is the most common use, but it is also commonly defined as the purchase price plus planned capital improvements, the value determined by an appraiser, or the expected value when development or value-add is complete. Even different lenders, or the same lender on different properties, will calculate LTV in different ways. Obviously, these various metrics can be easily used to make a deal appear to be less leveraged than it actually is.

Make sure you understand how the loan-to-value ratio is calculated and think about what needs to occur for it to be true. What is a "safe" loan to value? That depends on your perspective. In a stable market, LTV describes how much value can be lost before the equity is wiped out and the lender beings to absorb a loss of principal. In reality, property sales in down markets may not bring enough buyers to provide a solid market value. If the planned value-add hasn't been added or the development hasn't been developed, the LTV may be irrelevant if it's measured based on completed value. Despite all these caveats, most institutional investors set LTV limits around 50% to 60% for core or core-plus allocations investing in stabilized properties. More opportunistic investments may have debt in the 70% to 80% range or higher.

DCR & Debt Yield

Like the LTV, the Debt Coverage Ratio ("DCR", also known as the Debt Service Coverage Ratio ("DSCR") is simple in concept but squishy in practice. Conceptually, the goal is to estimate how much cash flow cushion a deal has by dividing net operating income (NOI, or cash available to pay the loan) by the loan payments. If the property generates significantly more cash than is needed to pay the loan, you can feel more comfortable that distress will be avoided; at least until the debt matures.

$$Debt\ Coverage\ Ratio\ (DCR) = \frac{\text{Net Operating Income (NOI)}}{\text{Loan Payment}}$$

Without focusing too much on accounting conventions, NOI is the income available after all operating expenses and recurring capital, but before one-time capital or extraordinary events. The accounts used to calculate NOI are moderately consistent across companies, however there are a few variations. As an example, some companies pull partnership-related items (partnership taxes, audit, or other similar expenses) below the NOI line.

Capex is an area of particular uncertainty. There can be some flexibility with the allocation of some kinds of recurring capital expenditures to be either above or below the line. Keep in mind that "industry standard" levels of recurring capital expenditures can significantly underestimate the actual expense of maintaining properties at a stable and competitive level. If projections are made based on industry standards or norms, make sure the operator has experience running similar properties or has other logic backing up their assumptions, so they won't be surprised by actual expenses.

Last, like the concept of value discussed in the LTV section, NOI may not be stable at a property due to value add or market trends. Is the NOI based on historical income and expenses? Projected first-year operations? Post-renovation projections?

Debt service payments for fixed rate loans are typically calculated based on a fully amortizing payment at the actual note rate. For floating rate loans, a "floor" or "stressed" rate is picked above the current market rate to ensure the property can withstand some interest rate movement without being forced into distress. This stressed rate varies from lender to lender and may be lower if a financial instrument is used to hedge against or cap rate risk.

In low-interest rate environments, some fixed-rate lenders set an additional DCR test based on a stressed rate which is higher than the current coupon, similar to that in a floating rate transaction. If rates go up, the thinking goes, can the property generate sufficient cash flow for another lender to refinance the existing loan? Although frustrating for borrowers when rates are low, this is an eminently reasonable concern.

The debt yield is used by some lenders, particularly life companies and securitized lenders, in addition to or in lieu of the stressed DCR to compare a property's earning potential to the loan balance. The debt yield is the NOI divided by the loan amount. Lenders will set a minimum level, for instance 8%, which will be used as a constraint on the amount they are willing to lend against a property. Like the stressed DCR, lenders look at the debt yield as another rule of thumb to limit maturity risk – the risk that when the loan comes due the property will be unable to refinance out the current loan in full. Lower debt yields indicate a riskier deal.

$$Debt\ Yield\ (\%) = \frac{Net\ Operating\ Income\ (NOI)}{Loan\ Amount} X\ 100$$

Lenders may use multiple DCR tests that need to be achieved in stages to ensure the anticipated business plan is being achieved. Like the LTV, understand the thought process behind the calculation rather than focusing just on the output. For stabilized properties, DCRs in the 1.25x-1.5x range are common. For value-add transactions DCRs can shrink to or near the 1.0x cash-flow breakeven level. Deals with this profile count on the value-add occurring to create a cash flow cushion and will have less room for error if the market takes a turn for the worse.

CHAPTER 8: MARKET FORECASTS & ECONOMIC STORYTELLING

"Prediction is very difficult, especially about the future." – Niels Bohr

Valuing real estate is storytelling about future cash flows, and forecasting cash flows is storytelling about future real estate market conditions. Valuations and modeling are only as good as their assumptions. As the saying goes, "garbage in, garbage out".

For better or worse, market forecasts make or break investment decisions. Small changes to rent growth assumptions often tip the scales for or against deals. Given their importance, just as it is worth understanding the role DCF valuations and modeling play in real estate investment, it's worth understanding how forecasts are used to drive these valuations.

As discussed previously, GPs usually value real estate using a pro forma investment model which uses these key assumptions as inputs to forecast cash flow and values at various points in the future until the property is sold. With most real estate, there are surprisingly few moving parts to the valuation. After deals close it's not uncommon for me to talk to other GPs in my industry about our respective valuations and assumptions. I'm often surprised at how similar our conclusions are on deals, despite coming up with entirely separate valuations from the ground up. By similar, I mean within 0.1%-0.2% on $50M to $75M deals, essentially identical considering all the uncertainties involved. With competition this tight, a minor change in assumptions could easily be the difference between having the highest valuation or not.

The two assumptions that usually have the largest impact on valuation for stabilized deals are rent growth and exit cap. Other assumptions, like loss to lease or line item expenses are either transitory (so don't impact the sale price and thus the valuation as much) or have a smaller impact on total returns. For the purposes of illustration, let's discuss rent growth forecasts and their impact on investing strategy.

By convention, investors underwrite rent growth within a very tight range. Confirmation bias is rampant, and deviation from the norm requires exceptional justification. If we look at average rent growth over the course of a five year period for instance (to smooth out noise from unique circumstances), my experience is that most investors underwrite growth somewhere between 2.5% and 4% on the majority of deals. Why? 2% to 2.5% is a pretty common baseline inflation assumption, and if you're underwriting rents to grow slower than inflation, you're anticipating rental decreases in real dollars. There's nothing inherently wrong with that from a mechanical valuation point of view, but few investors are buying real estate with the expectation that things are getting worse rather than better over the medium term, at least not in normal market circumstances. Anything over 4% gets tough to justify because 1) it just sounds big, and 2) few third party market forecasting like to predict big increases over long periods so it's hard to find data to support those assumptions.

In reality though, net rental income falls outside this range more often than it falls within it. To test this hypothesis, I reviewed historical data about the average annual change in multifamily net rental income (using the proxy of rents net of concessions and vacancy) for consecutive five-year time periods in multiple submarkets within a major region going back in some submarkets as far as 30 years. Average rent growth over any given 5-year period in that data set was between 2.5% and 4% less than 15% of the time. (I would love to perform a more formal analysis of historical actual and forecasted rents… any market forecast firms up for sharing an analysis of their data publicly?) My non-scientific conclusion is that we, as an industry generally, systematically and significantly underestimate the volatility of market conditions. Key real estate assumptions are not normally distributed, they are full of "fat tail" distributions and noise. We pick reasonable sounding assumptions because they are saleable, not because they have a high likelihood of being true.

So where do these assumptions come from? The GP of course can use any assumptions they please. This is an area that requires self-control, some appropriately timed courage, an understanding of what your investors will be willing to accept, and a healthy dose of humility. With aggressive forecasts it would be easy to justify buying every deal, which might be ok at some points in the cycle but will inevitably be a problem for both investors and the GP in the long run. On the flip side, it is easy to be scared of your own shadow, afraid to take any risks, and to sit on the sidelines never doing deals. This of course is a great way to avoid losing your investors' money, but a lousy way to run a business. As Keynes reminds us, "In the long run, we are all dead." I have known, and at times been part of, companies near both extremes. Threading the appropriate line between them, and taking into account market conditions, is the art of successful real estate investing.

The actual assumptions used are the source of much discussion in investment committee meetings and around the hallways. Different parts of the same companies tend to fall in predictable camps – the investment group is often optimistic (they are usually compensated based on volume), while the operations group is often conservative (they are incentivized to beat a budget). The main considerations actually used to define these assumptions are usually:

- What is likely to be true?
- What can be justified with third party market forecasts?
- What is necessary to buy the deal?
- What will investors accept as realistic?

To address the first two items, third party market forecasts are a critical tool used to understand the market, support assumptions, and ultimately buy deals. Some companies pick a single forecast group to follow and use the data precisely and religiously. Others cherry pick forecasts to their liking from different forecasters. Few though, can get away without any third-party support. This unsurprisingly creates strong demand for market research and strong competition between the research firms to be the data provider of choice.

In order to be successful, economic forecasting firms need to have a product people want to buy. This means it needs to be, first and foremost, credible.

Accuracy is good too, but it's hard to objectively evaluate the track record of most groups. Credibility is what allows people to reference your work in support of their assumptions. Years later, it also provides plausible deniability to GPs, absolving them of blame when the predictions turn out to have been wildly inaccurate.

To create credibility, forecast firms hire rooms full of PHD economists and mathematicians to create complex forecasting models. Verisimilitude is a smart sales strategy. Who wants to argue with a room full of nerds? Nobody. These models are mostly regression models at heart. A regression model works as follows:

1. Gather a lot of historical data on the real estate and economy (rents, vacancies, construction pipeline, GDP, wages, employment... you name it)

2. Have your room of PHDs create a mathematical story about the how these things interact, a beautifully complex tale told about correlation and causation. (As an oversimplified example, if new construction increases office supply by 2% next year and all else stays constant, rents will fall 5% the following year)

3. Based on the current set of economic inputs, have the model forecast how the world will look over the next few years.

These econometric storytelling models are fascinating and can be very valuable as long as they're used with an appropriate degree of caution. Some of the forecasts are "black boxes", but some provide quite a bit of valuable information about the underlying inputs so you can better understand the complex factors impacting the market. The latter category is the most helpful because even if you are skeptical about the accuracy of the result, they help you understand the potential risk factors and economic drivers influencing the market. As an example, if you know there is both an employment boom and a development boom, you may draw a different investment conclusion then you would knowing that employment is stagnant and the development pipeline is dry. Either of these scenarios might have identical rent growth forecasts for very different reasons.

What econometric models aren't good at, like the rest of us, is foreseeing the unforeseeable. Sudden downturns caused (or perhaps just triggered) by different circumstances than the last downturn don't show up in regression analyses based on past data. These larger macro events cause big shifts in demand for real estate and are usually what surprise investors. In this sense, economic forecasting provides the same type of service for investors that TSA checkpoints provide for travelers; safety theater.

Once, when reviewing the options for economic forecast subscriptions, I was involved with a series of demos and interviews of some of the major services. The salesperson from one prominent firm, who will remain unnamed, had a detailed and aggressive pitch about how his product was backed by the smartest analysts, had the most sophisticated model, and a long track record of accurate forecasting. When we asked him about his forecasts prior to the great recession and if he would be willing to share those reports, his response was, "well... nobody saw THAT coming!"

Although they don't like to admit it, it's hard for market forecasting firms to sell bearish forecasts. Clients are typically equity and debt investors looking for a confirmation of their assumptions enabling them to do more deals. It's tough to justify spending tens of thousands of dollars for forecasts that can't be used to support your business, so there is strong market pressure to have a rosy outlook. Forecasting firms also aren't motivated to predict strong market movements, either up or down, even if they have good reason to believe them. The most typical rent growth forecasts in normal market conditions show a year or two of above market growth (remember - think positive!) followed by a reversion to steady growth in the out years of the forecast. Some submarkets will deviate due to unique circumstances, but that's the most common prediction. Years after the fact, it's easier for the sales team to explain a market trend forecast that was wrong due to a sudden downturn than it is to explain why you predicted big rent declines that never materialized.

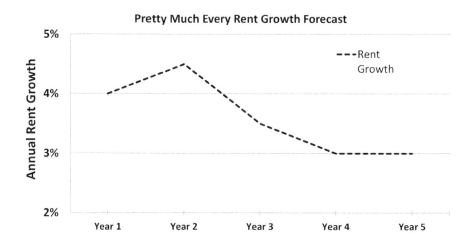

There are admittedly some market forecasters who's claim to fame are their predictions of one or more downturns. Perhaps some are lucky, some are good, and some are "perma-bears" who make a living by pointing out potential catastrophes around every corner (the ones who predicted 10 of the past 5 recessions successfully). You won't usually find these experts on industry panels – being a downer is a tough gig. Still, it's worth hearing out the arguments on both sides and it's good to have some contrarians out there to help fight groupthink and to keep things entertaining.

As long as your expectations for market forecasts are realistic, they can be a valuable tool to help understand market trends and risks. If you take their long-term forecasts as a foregone conclusion, however, be prepared for some unexpected surprises.

I don't mean to be too hard on economic forecasters. After all, they have an extraordinarily difficult job. Forecasting the future of the American economy and trends in the commercial real estate world with any precision is a lot to ask of anyone, and it is always frustrating to deal with armchair quarterbacks critiquing your work after the fact. I also suspect most economists dislike the sales pressure inherent in the business. A colleague's company recently hired economists from a major economic forecasting team into their direct real estate investment company. The team was supposedly looking for an opportunity to share their actual predictions without pressure to modify it from an internal sales and management group. Like many businesses, this one has its quirks, which is fine as long as your expectations are realistic.

Not all forecasts are quite as fuzzy as those mentioned above. Interest rate forecasts, as an example, can be obtained from looking at forward curves in the bond market to understand where the "market" is predicting interest rates to be at certain points in the future. I like these forecasts a bit more than econometric forecasts, not because they can't be wrong (they definitely can), but because I feel better knowing that they are the result of real people investing real money based on an expected outcome. Accurate or not, that skin in the game makes me feel better.

Some forecasts of development pipelines are taken from actual entitlement applications with cities for new properties at various stages of the development process. These forecasts are helpful, because they tend to be an accurate picture of where the pipeline stands at any given time. In many markets, long entitlement timelines make these reliable in the near future. Over the longer term, or during periods of market distress, these pipelines can evaporate quickly as new developments stop making economic sense. Again, not perfect, but helpful due to the reliable data set.

The unfortunate reality is that life is uncertain. Believing too much in any forecast is a recipe for disaster. It's worthwhile spending time thinking about the most likely outcome, but far more important to look at a range of outcomes. Baseline investment scenarios always seem to make sense, but it's critical to make sure you're comfortable with the risk profile of your investment across a variety of possible economic outcomes.

Richard Feynman once said, "The first rule is that you must not fool yourself, and you are the easiest person to fool." Few people like to admit the extent of our uncertainty about the future, but accepting it is the first step toward making better investment decisions. The only certainty is that your forecasts will be wrong. The only question is in what way they will turn out to have been wrong. If you can accept this, watching the uncertainty unfold can become a Zen form of entertainment. Be the uncertainty. Feel it flow through your model and into your conclusions.

Make sure you diversify too.

CHAPTER 9: CRAFTING & EXECUTING YOUR STRATEGY

"The test of the machine is the satisfaction it gives you. There isn't any other test. If the machine produces tranquility it's right. If it disturbs you it's wrong until either the machine or your mind is changed." - Robert M. Pirsig, Zen and the Art of Motorcycle Maintenance: An Inquiry Into Values

Setting an Allocation

The first step in crafting a practical private real estate investment portfolio is picking your allocation to the strategy. Unfortunately, there is no clean and quantitative way to decide what asset allocation is objectively correct. Like most of you probably have, I have searched online for information about asset allocation and found a wealth of articles and calculators on the topic, some of which might be valuable, some not. You ultimately need to decide for yourself what is appropriate given your personal circumstances. As you consider this, take into account your need for liquidity, age, allocation of other investments, risk tolerance, and tax implications. You should definitely discuss your decision with your financial and tax advisers. Whatever method you use to come to your conclusion, think carefully about it. Once you invest in private real estate, you're stuck with it for a long time so it's tough to change your mind without paying a steep price. In rough times, your real estate investments can hang over you like the Sword of Damocles; the hair trigger riding on every lease expiration and tenant bankruptcy. Investments' hedonic value is an important consideration! As Cicero said, "Does not Dionysius seem to have made it sufficiently clear that there can be nothing happy for the person over whom some fear always looms?", something to keep in mind when contemplating your allocation.

Based on my conversations with private investors, allocations to the space are commonly in the 0% to 25% range. Industry insiders tend to have a much higher allocation of their net worth in real estate, but they often don't have a choice (in order to meet co-invest requirements) and are forced to tolerate more risk and volatility than your average investor probably would want. Plus, some of them are just real estate junkies and can't help themselves. Real estate is not an all-encompassing addiction I would recommend for most prudent investors.

Once you pick your allocation, it's time to evaluate if and how you can effectively invest it while maintaining a diversified portfolio. Here's an example of this problem for illustration: You have $1,100,000 in investable assets. You want to invest in a syndicated deal with $1,000,000 minimums. You can do it, but you would have the vast majority of your capital tied up in a single property... probably not something a prudent investor would do regardless of the quality of the opportunity.

So, the question is, what investments will achieve your goals without taking on too much concentration risk? Your investable portfolio (and subsequent allocation to real estate) is the limiting factor. In addition to the number of investments, you also need to consider the inherent diversification within each investment. As an example, a single REIT index fund can cover a broad spectrum of property types, geographies, and parts of the capital stack in a single investment. In comparison, it may take many separate investments in single-property syndications to achieve a minimal level of comfort that you are avoiding concentration risk. The goal of all this is to decide what types of investments work for you, and how many of each you need to make to create an optimal real estate portfolio.

This process is unique to each investor and there are no right or wrong answers. Because this is a bit theoretical, let's look at a practical example, shown in the table below. The goal of this exercise is to determine how large of an investment portfolio you would need to be able to achieve an acceptable level of diversification using the investments discussed in this book. You can do the math for yourself based on your own situation using the same process. This is how it works:

- Each column in the table shows a different type of real estate investment, with headings at the top.
- The first row represents the minimum number of investments (if you were to invest only in that product type) that you would need in order to have a sufficiently diversified real estate portfolio. Obviously, this number is the result of personal preference so will vary depending on your risk appetite.
- The next row shows a typical minimum investment size allowed for that type of product. This varies by operator.
- Now, on the next row, the minimum number of investments is multiplied by the minimum investment size to estimate the minimum real estate allocation size that would achieve acceptable diversification.
- Finally, on the last rows, we calculate how large an investment portfolio would be needed to achieve sufficient diversification while also keeping your real estate allocation within an acceptable percentage of your total investments. I run this based on three scenarios; 5%, 15%, and 25% - all within the realm of normalcy.

	REIT Fund	Individual REITs	Private Fund	Crowdfunding Syndications	Traditional Syndications
Minimum # of Investments	1	5	2	10	10
Minimum Investment Size	$1,000	$1,000	$250,000	$25,000	$100,000
Minimum Allocation	$1,000	$5,000	$500,000	$250,000	$1,000,000
Minimum Portfolio Size (25% Allocation)	$4,000	$20,000	$2,000,000	$1,000,000	$4,000,000
Minimum Portfolio Size (15% Allocation)	$6,667	$33,333	$3,333,333	$1,666,667	$6,666,667
Minimum Portfolio Size (5% Allocation)	$20,000	$100,000	$10,000,000	$5,000,000	$20,000,000

So... if you have $2,000,000 in investable assets, want to keep your real estate allocation at or below 25%, and want to build a real estate portfolio entirely from private syndications, you probably won't be able to do it without taking on too much risk. Either you would have to take on too much concentration risk (because you have too few individual investments in your real estate allocation) or you would have to take allocation risk (because you have too much of your portfolio tied up in real estate). On the other hand, you could probably come up with an acceptable portfolio by investing in more diversified funds with $250,000 minimums.

Of course, the real world is much messier. Most investors put money in a variety of product types and have to deal with re-allocating their money as investments mature. The point here is to think about how much and what types of risk you are willing to accept, then plan your real estate allocation around that.

This example clearly shows why REITs are the most effective investment vehicle for most investors. Even though investment minimums may sound reasonably modest for syndications, building a sufficiently diversified real estate portfolio can quickly balloon the minimum portfolio size beyond the reach of many investors. Even with our 10-investment example, investors are still accepting much more concentration risk than many REIT investments would provide.

This table also illustrates a real advantage to crowdfunded investments – their smaller minimum investments. In addition to simplifying the investment process, smaller investment minimums open the syndicated private real estate world to a much larger group of investors simply by requiring much smaller total net worth to achieve an acceptable level of risk.

Keep in mind, this is not advice about your particular situation. It's up to you to decide, with full awareness, what level of concentration risk and investment risk you are willing to tolerate. Even for large investors, there is every reason to spread your allocation across a variety of product types, mixing REITs with funds and individual syndications to give your portfolio its own unique texture.

Investment Strategy & Risk Profile

With an allocation in hand, it's time to think about your strategy for investing that allocation. Real estate isn't a commodity. An allocation full of moderately leveraged income generating property will perform very differently through market cycles than an allocation stuffed with ground-up development or land deals. Spreading out your bets within the real estate asset class is critical to avoiding concentration risk with a single operator, market, product type, or investment strategy.

Within the real estate asset class, deals are often categorized in the following four very broad categories to define risk: core, core plus, value-add, and opportunistic. There is some overlap between the categories in practice since there is no perfect definition of each. Their breadth means a detail-oriented investor could sub-categorize much more, but they at least give investors a quick idea of the level of risk they're exposed to in a transaction or fund.

Investment Strategies

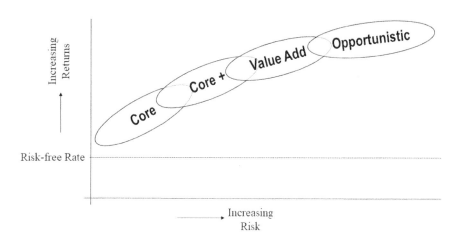

Core

The lowest risk category of property, core, are well located in the largest major markets. The buildings are new and well-built, tenants are high quality, and they avoid risk from lease rollover concentration. Managers put core properties on the front cover of their brochure. Core property is like IBM; it's tough for an investment manager to get fired for investing in it.

Core is generally the domain of the institutional investor (pension funds, insurance companies, or REITs) because its lower leverage and volatility makes it tough for syndicators and other private equity investors to raise private money and generate returns high enough to earn a promote. Current income typically provides 70% to 80% of total returns (Mancuso 2011). Levered returns in stable market conditions are often in the high single digits. They are typically purchased with low leverage and a long-term investment horizon.

Although core deals seem like they shouldn't lose money, keep in mind that they are not completely safe investments. Extremely low cap rates can mean that small changes in industry cap rates (due to increases in interest rates for instance) can have a larger percentage effect on values for core deals than their higher-cap rate brethren. Also, high quality markets are subject to extreme changes in rents (up and down) during market cycles just like inferior markets. The concept of mean-reversion is particularly important here – although markets can outperform or underperform for long periods due to structural changes, C markets can't underperform A markets forever. If they did, rents would become infinitely expensive in A markets. At some point, when a market outperforms enough (from the perspective of a landlord collecting rent of course), high rents justify new development or tenants simply move somewhere cheaper. The point of all this is to say that investing in the nice part of town is not necessarily a lower risk proposition from a rental-rate risk perspective than investing in the rough part of town.

Core Plus

Taking a small step up the investment risk spectrum brings us to the core-plus category. Core-plus deals are almost core deals, but for one reason or another don't quite fit in the core category. Perhaps a well-designed property is in a prime location but it's too old for institutional investors. Maybe a newly constructed property is in an emerging neighborhood that makes core investors nervous. These properties rarely require significant amounts of capital investment or offer an opportunity for much rent movement. Core plus deals usually offer slightly higher returns than core deals, justified by their slightly higher risk profile. How much of a premium depends on the market and capital market conditions, but a 2%-3% higher IRR over a medium to long term hold in comparison to core deals is not uncommon. In normal conditions, this might mean levered returns in the low-teens. Many institutional investors such as pension funds or real estate managers have a core-plus allocation or product offering, but returns on core plus deals, like core deals, are often too thin for syndicators to generate good projected promotes. If done right, core-plus investing should still be pretty boring.

Value-Add

Things start to get a little more fun in the value-add space. Investors in these deals are looking for under-utilized properties with the potential to be improved. This vision is usually realized by making a significant capital investment; upgrading an old exterior to give the property a fresh new look or reinventing interior spaces to appeal to a new tenant profile or justify higher rents from existing tenants. Fixing up a property can give it new life, taking it up a level in the quality spectrum, perhaps from a "B" to an "A-". Value-add deals are justified by looking at upside rental comps, deciding how much money would need to be invested to compete with them, and determining if the higher rents and associated higher property value will justify the investment.

Value-add usually refers to deals that require an investment in capital to physically upgrade the property but can sometimes refer to deals that have operational risk or are under-managed. Perhaps a property is run down after a period of financial distress or it has a large tenant rollover risk. The operational risk is too high to be considered core-plus, but the risk profile is not scary enough to justify an "opportunistic" label, so these deals fall into the value-add category.

In exchange for this additional risk, investors demand higher returns from value-add deals, often another 2%-4% more than core-plus deals, putting them in the mid-teens return profile. Holding periods are often shorter and might involve alignment of a shorter-term business plan with shorter term floating rate financing. This can provide flexibility and lower prepayment penalties but increases risk from deteriorating market conditions and capital markets if the investment climate shifts mid-investment. Although many institutional investors have a value-add allocation, the return profile is high enough that it works for many syndicate investors as well. Since syndicate investor volume is more volatile, this space can suffer from floods of capital specifically targeting value-add deals, driving down return spreads in comparison to core-plus deals (which are usually too boring to sell well). In theory, returns for value-add deals are materially higher than core-plus, but stretched underwriting assumptions can compress this premium in practice.

Opportunistic

The most interesting, and riskiest, profile of real estate deals are described as opportunistic. Land entitlement, ground-up development, adaptive re-use, re-tenanting, and other similar deals all fall into this category. Opportunistic deals often don't have enough in-place cash flow to cover significant amounts of debt, so in addition to real estate risk, they can involve risk from financial engineering and are particularly susceptible to timing and path dependence issues. If the market takes a turn for the worse, all the opportunistic deals may tank at once, even if they are spread out across multiple operators, geographies, and product types. I believe that opportunistic transactions have a place in a well-diversified portfolio, but I think many investors over-allocate to the space because they underestimate the risks involved.

Operators love opportunistic deals. It's easier to sell a deal with an exciting story, and investors are less likely to object to larger fees and promotes when pro forma returns are higher and when operators are adding value through the entitlement, development, or construction process. It's often true that operators can bring substantial value to opportunistic deals through relationships or experience that makes them uniquely qualified to execute on an opportunity. Still, market movements may overwhelm the influence of even the most skilled operator, so picking an experienced company is a necessary but not sufficient requirement for investing in the space. Also recall that operators are incentivized to be risk-seeking, so opportunistic deals are a chance for GPs to roll the dice and hope for a big payoff.

Along with outsized risk can come outsized returns. These deals require a significant return premium over value-add deals, and are often marketed at over 20% IRRs, although the multiples can be more modest due to shorter hold periods. In reality, the uncertainty involved with these deals can make financial modeling tough so it's best not to lose sight of underwriting basics.

A Chinese proverb is said to have advised, "May you live in interesting times". If you relate to this, opportunistic investments deserve your consideration. When they go well, they can be home runs. When they go badly, they can go very badly. Either way they will be memorable. If you participate in the space, brace yourself for excitement; both good and bad.

Finding and Reviewing Offerings

Over time, reviewing and evaluating offerings becomes routine. Common tricks and traps can be avoided, and you can easily determine if deal values are generally in line with market comps. The goal of reviewing offerings is to make sure you're not doing something stupid… at least not something that can be easily avoided.

The closest thing in today's world to a public marketplace for offerings are the crowdfunding sites. Being able to evaluate an offering alone isn't enough though. If your goal is a diversified real estate allocation across geography and asset classes, you're unlikely to get that by passively waiting for offerings to show up in your inbox. You need to actively search out and identify the operators you want to invest with and make sure you are on their distribution lists for potential offerings. This will take an active search on your part. Since securities regulations prevent managers from general solicitation, identifying potential investments isn't just a mouse click away. I'm confident that someday it will be as easy to hop online to search for industrial investments in Colorado as it is to search for flights there, but as of this writing we are a long way from that scenario.

Unfortunately, because the space is so new, the quality of operators and deals are not universally great. Many of the highest quality operators don't raise money through these sites because the effort involved (additional legal complexity, longer timelines, and risk from the addition of many new small investors) isn't worthwhile. For established operators doing larger transactions, crowdfunding platforms can only raise a small portion of the equity for a transaction. Why would they pay fees to go through the effort and risk of crowdfunding when they probably have more than enough equity available from their existing investor base? When crowdfunding gains traction, this dynamic will inevitably change, and I hope it does soon for the sake of both investors and sponsors.

Even though crowdfunding sites aren't comprehensive, they are a good place to quickly review a lot of offerings. If you aren't familiar with a market niche, it is worth signing up to get a better sense of deal terms and metrics.

Funds offer the simplest method for putting together a diversified private portfolio, but if you want to build a bespoke portfolio your only real option is to use a bottom-up approach:

1. Decide what you want to invest in and where
2. Find operators who specialize in those investments
3. Pick deals and write checks

Defining Your Investment Strategy (Picking Your Poison)

The unfortunate reality of investing is that timing is everything. Best-in-class operators struggle to make money with peak-market investments, and even mediocre operators look like geniuses when they nail the bottom of a downturn.

Timing real estate markets, if you believe you have the ability to, is mechanically easy for investors; it's just a buy/not buy decision. For operators though, it creates a real conundrum. Full service real estate companies can't easily turn on and off the spigot to various investment strategies without significant personnel and reputational costs. Likewise, lenders, architects, engineers, and other industry players tend to have slow moving corporate operations and cultures. Because changing investment strategies is so hard, the real estate industry is particularly susceptible to groupthink. Each year, transaction volume targets for employees are increased from the last, and prices increase incrementally. Investment return requirements are slightly looser than last year. Rent growth forecasts are slightly higher. Value-add premiums go up a bit. The bubble steadily inflates - until it doesn't. Something goes wrong, transaction volume freezes, employees are laid off, investors and lenders switch their settings to "risk off", and prices freefall.

Some investment companies regularly release a graphic showing a smooth sinusoidal curve along with commentary about where the industry stands in the current cycle. My practical experience has been that markets don't roll smoothly past inflection points on the way up and down. Downturns happen suddenly and violently, followed by steady incremental growth as surviving market participants creep out from their bunkers and tentatively re-explore their shattered dystopian world. Momentum builds, rents climb, a few good deals are harvested, and before you know it the industry is living large and everyone is a winner. Until the next implosion. Rather than a nice smooth process, the real estate cycle is characterized by steadily accelerating prices and volume followed by an abrupt disruption. The question "What inning are we in?" is invariably asked at every session of every industry conference, and while it's clichéd, it's a better description of the cycle than the sine curve. The game proceeds steadily, with perhaps some excitement at the end, then just stops... until the next one starts.

Because of this industry inertia, I don't think it's as hard to identify irrational investment behavior in real estate as it is in other more liquid markets. Boom times are recognizable by the lavish parties thrown by brokers and great investment opportunities are usually easy to find when financing and equity raising is impossible. For a good indicator of the state of the market, look to the real estate industrial complex – the army of real estate industry players (lenders, attorneys, architects, service providers, consultants, etc.) who make money from transactions but have little personal cash at stake in investments. This REIC helps provide momentum to the market and its size is inversely related to the quality of investments available. When industry conference attendance is at all-time highs, I'd recommend being judicious about the type of investments you make.

In a notable pre-crisis boom, one of the senior partners in my firm had some unsolicited advice in one of our weekly "all hands" meetings, which was more or less the following: "If you aren't absolutely crushing it right now, you should find a new career. Immediately. Things will never be better than they are now." He and his partners believed it too; they sold the company shortly thereafter, right before the market tanked. At the trough of the crisis, they took the company back to rebuild it in time for the next boom.

Many of real estate's current elder statesmen and stateswomen made their profits and built their track records in the days of the Resolution Trust Corporation (RTC). The RTC was a government owned asset management company that liquidated the assets (many of which were real estate) during the savings and loan crisis of the 1980s. (Davidson 2005) Industry veterans get misty eyed as they wistfully recall the era of incredible "can't lose" investments, obvious even then in the middle of a crisis. These apparent and lasting opportunities have been less prevalent in the years since. In the great recession, piles of money were raised to buy distressed opportunities that barely materialized because banks weren't forced by regulators in many cases to dispose of distressed assets. Markets and pricing snapped back much quicker than experienced market participants expected. Opportunities existed but capitalizing on them required access to capital in the midst of an effectively frozen investment market. Perhaps this faster dynamic is the new norm, perhaps not.

Despite my belief that real estate cycles are not as sudden and unexpected as those in more liquid markets, I am still skeptical about my own skill at outright market timing. Rather than jumping in and out of the asset class, plan to allocate to it permanently. Even for a perfectly prescient market timer, timing the entry and exit of an entire allocation based on market conditions is impractical, particularly because LPs don't control sell decisions. Research shows that while stock fund investors are generally willing to ride out market cycles, alternative investors chase returns across alternative classes, actively trying to time the market, and they pay a performance price as a result. John Rekenthaler of Morningstar writes, "If fund investors truly viewed alternatives as a necessary part of the portfolio, as the yang to conventional funds' yin, they would accept their performance downturns as patiently as they accept stock market declines. But investors don't. They think of alternatives as another flavor of sector fund-- an optional slice that makes the owner (or the adviser who made the recommendation) look smarter than the everyday rabble if the fund performs well. If the fund does not perform well, then it's off to Plan B. Or Plan C." (Rekenthaler 2015)

Taking these factors into account, I would advise against making sudden moves with your investment allocation. Going from zero to full allocation will make it difficult to avoid vintage risk / cycle risk (the risk that you are getting in at the wrong point in the cycle, when nearly all deals will do badly) and tougher to spread out the timing of dispositions. If the goal is to stay allocated over the long term, it is helpful to have a series of investments rolling over regularly and being replaced by new investments so not all of your allocation runs the risk of being sold into a downturn or bought at cyclical peaks. To the extent you want to tinker with your allocation, you can then change where you reinvest your proceeds. What industry indexes can't take into account is the risk profile of individual investments, something you will be actively choosing if you are picking each investment, or to a lesser extent by choosing a fund. Instead of making an invest vs. don't invest decision about the industry, change your thinking to deciding between "risk on" or "risk off". If you time the market, do it by being contrarian about your risk profile. If you're seeing signs of market froth, pick deals with less leverage and less risky business plans. If you're going to roll the dice on a riskier profile deal, do it in the depths of a downturn – when financing is tough to get, vacancy is at cyclical highs, prices are well below replacement costs, and preferably with an established operator and appropriate leverage.

Real Estate Market Efficiency

While we're on the topic of cycles, it's worth discussing the related topic of market efficiency. Much ink has been spilled about the efficiency of financial markets, and the debate in many cases sounds more like a religious conflict than the geeky quarrel over data interpretation it really is. In 2013, the Nobel committee split the prize for economics between Eugene Fama (the father of efficient markets) and Robert Shiller (a noted efficient markets critic). Apparently, the committee couldn't come to a conclusion either.

Fama describes efficiency as "the simple statement that security prices reflect all available information" (Fama 1991). In the real estate world, it is inherently hard to measure "true" value, for reasons discussed previously, so it lends itself awkwardly to measurements of efficiency, but the question of whether the real estate market is efficient is a critical practical matter for all real estate investors, whether huge or tiny. If markets are efficient, focusing on fees and diversifying your allocation should be top priorities. If markets are inefficient, picking sponsors and timing the market are important strategies.

As a wayward engineer, I have a natural proclivity for clean and quantitative descriptions of the world, and I immediately loved the elegance of the efficient markets hypothesis (EMH) when I was introduced to it in business school. EMH, Capital Asset Pricing Model (CAPM), the efficient frontier... whether you're a believer or not, they're an undeniably graceful interpretation of an otherwise messy world. Once out of the halls of academia though, I lived the reality of a market most people describe as inefficient and have witnessed firsthand the dynamics of buyers, sellers and the REIC. My priors were strongly in favor of efficiency, but it became increasingly hard to reconcile them with the untidy reality I was living.

My personal opinions have migrated over time to a middle ground on the efficiency question. Most of the transactions I work on involve institutional or at least professional owners or advisers and the sales process and transaction process is highly systematized to take into account price, terms, and buyer credibility to generate maximum value with minimum risk to the seller. Above around $10,000,000, transactions are typically brokered, or a standard sales process is used by the seller to mimic the brokerage process. Many institutional investors require their GP partners to sell properties through brokers to ensure they receive full market value. The resulting market for these deals is surprisingly efficient. Experienced buyers can usually estimate, within a few percentage points, where a deal will ultimately trade. Truly "below market" deals negotiated directly with a clueless seller are extremely rare. It's possible to tie up deals off market, but sellers know the value of their own property too and will want to be compensated for skipping the full marketing process so they can convince their investors that they haven't done something stupid without testing the market. Internally, we refer to this phenomenon as the "off market premium", not something worth paying unless you care more about the story than the investment.

At the same time, it's impossible to ignore the messiness of the system. As a seller, it's not uncommon to have to choose between two buyers, one with a higher price but lower credibility and another with a great reputation but a lower price. Occasionally, a buyer's exchange requirements will make them desperate to avoid taxes and create a windfall for the seller. Other times, deals become shopworn after a few unlucky busted escrows and sellers have to accept much less than anyone would have guessed to get the transaction closed.

So where do I stand on efficiency? An article in Institutional Investor described this phenomenon beautifully as being "efficiently inefficient" (Pedersen 2015). The commercial real estate market has just enough inefficiency to support specialized investors who can benefit from strong reputations and market expertise. Perhaps this is a self-serving point of view, and perhaps it is also true.

Whenever I see offerings boasting about an amazing below/off market deal, I approach them with a healthy dose of skepticism, and I recommend you do too. The real money to be made in real estate when the market isn't in distress is in picking the right asset class and deal at the right time and executing the investment flawlessly, not in finding and exploiting oblivious sellers.

Identifying and Evaluating Managers

Because securities regulations limit managers' ability to make investments publicly available to potential investors, you will need to do some proactive work to identify managers in your target markets. This is a moderately frustrating process in an age of at-your-fingertips information, but here are a few suggestions to help you identify potential investment groups.

If you work with an investment adviser, your first call should be to them. The registered investment adviser (RIA) business has been undergoing a significant migration from in-house commission-based sales brokers to fee-only financial advisers. Traditional brokerage firms rarely sold clients real estate private equity products, but this shift has freed advisers to recommend a broader variety of products to clients, including real estate. Although not all groups do it, some RIAs see a wide range of offerings, work closely with multiple real estate operators, and may have negotiated attractive terms on behalf of their clients.

Nearly all experienced operators are actively involved in one or more industry associations specific to their market niche. Attending these industry conferences will provide both an attendee list (a great place to source investment managers) and some good sessions to learn more about the asset class. The following associations are popular and draw a wide selection of people from their respective industries, but this list is by no means comprehensive:

- Urban Land Institute (ULI) www.uli.org: Multiple asset classes, focused generally on developers.
- National Multi Housing Council (NMHC) www.nmhc.org: Multifamily specific association.
- Commercial Real Estate Development Association (NAIOP) www.naiop.org: Commercial real estate, mostly office and industrial.
- International Council of Shopping Centers (ICSC) www.icsc.org: Retail specific association.

We have already identified crowdfunding websites as a valuable source of example transactions and industry information. The crowdfunding industry is very dynamic, with a lot of corporate turnover. Rather than list sites here and risk being immediately outdated, I recommend you use your favorite search engine to explore the crowdfunding universe. You will have plenty of options to choose from!

Here are a few other suggestions for ways to identify potential managers:

Networking with other investors: A good way to hear about potential investment companies, and perhaps more importantly, a great way to get feedback about good and bad experiences with those companies.

Attorneys & accountants: Attorneys who handle offering documents and purchase contracts for managers can be a good source of information, particularly for local groups. Many CPA firms also see a wide cross section of K1s come across their desks and may be a good source for referrals. Both may be hesitant to share candid information without a prior relationship because they don't want to provide investment advice to people they don't know. Getting information is easier when you are in general fact-finding mode.

Trade press: Although they can't advertise for specific investments, many investors do put out press releases to raise awareness of their company generally with both investors and potential industry counterparts. As discussed previously, being known as an active buyer and seller of property makes the acquisition process easier because it creates credibility with sellers and brokers. These press releases are just a few mouse clicks away for potential investors. By searching for transactions like those you're targeting, you will quickly come up with links to industry-specific publications with articles about investors who are active in the space. Set a search engine alert to automatically send news to your inbox related to your target deal profile.

Brokers: Investment sales brokers make it their job to know all major buyers and seller of real estate in their target product type and geography. They also have a good understanding of each company's investment style, history, and individual quirks. Major brokerage firms have teams in nearly every market who cover each product type. You can search for the appropriate groups from their main websites, here is a non-exhaustive list with a few of the majors:

- CBRE (www.cbre.com)
- Jones Lang LaSalle (www.us.jll.com)
- Cushman & Wakefield (www.cushmanwakefield.com)
- Newmark Grubb Night Frank (www.ngkf.com)
- Marcus & Millichap (www.marcusmillichap.com)

- Colliers International (www.colliers.com)
- Berkadia (www.berkadiarea.com)

Once you come up with a list of investment managers who fit your target profile, reach out directly (contact information is usually on their website) to get more information about the company and platform. People risk can't be avoided, but it can be managed. Ask for references and actually call them. Even better, ask other industry participants for their opinions. The real estate world remains very small and most operators in the same space have knowledge (and opinions) about their competitors. Evaluate them based on our previously discussed investor management criteria, and down-select your list to only those groups you would be willing to invest with. Ask to be added to their distribution list for future deals. It's a good idea to do your homework on groups far in advance of offerings so you are ready to decide quickly once an opportunity arises.

Whatever you do, don't make impulse investments in real estate. The acquisition process as a GP can seem like it unfolds in slow motion. Market trends take months or years to unfold, and decisions are predicated on weeks of careful analysis. My office is nearly always pleasant and subdued. Excitement and drama, at least in my company, is nearly always a bad thing. Investing as an LP should be the same way. Your careful homework on a manager and the asset class should mean that few things in a potential offering are surprising. If you're getting the hard sell, and don't feel completely confident, walk away. If you're getting the impression that the company spends more time marketing real estate than analyzing real estate, bail.

Let's take an example. As I mentioned, I'm signed up to receive offerings from a variety of crowdfunding sites and my inbox greeted me this morning with an email subject line along the following lines: "ONLY THREE SPOTS REMAIN: Off Market, Florida Multifamily, Target 15.32% IRR!" Even if the merits of the deal were legitimate (which they weren't, something I know because I was compelled to look at the overview for some inexplicable reason, perhaps because I felt the need to get riled up), I wouldn't invest only because of the email subject line:

- The call to action: B.S. If demand was overwhelming, they wouldn't be inundating relative strangers with marketing emails.

- All caps, with an exclamation mark: Are they hawking real estate or fake pharmaceuticals?
- "Off market": How much of a premium are they paying for it to convince the seller to transact without marketing the property?
- Florida: The land of speculation, foreclosure, endless developable land, and syndicated excess. See also; Texas and Nevada.
- 15.32% IRR: Forecasting a levered IRR to the hundredths place? Really?

Everything about this pitch is a red flag. Run, don't walk, from deals like this.

Spread your investments around as much as practically possible. Consider whether you can tolerate the complete meltdown of any of the companies you invest with. Real estate investment groups go under all the time with little warning to their investors; it's a fact of life. Spreading investments across multiple groups has the added benefit of providing some diversification through exposure to multiple platforms and strategies.

Game Theory & Courage

Part of what makes real estate fun is the interaction with other investors. Making investments is not a purely mathematical prediction game, it is done in the context of a competitive bidding market with other potential buyers. Each of these buyers has their own market forecasts, operational assumptions, equity sources, and investment strategies. As the selected buyer it's easy to second guess your strategy and question why you are willing to pay more for a property than a field of other qualified and experienced investors. This is the nature of the process though. Buying real estate requires investors to come up with an investment thesis and execute on it independent of the beliefs and opinions of others.

Incidentally, I try to avoid referring to being awarded a deal as "winning" it, although that's common jargon. My preferred word choice is more about superstition, a fear of the winner's curse, than anything else. I consider a deal "won" when it's sold for a profit. Until then, the investment is in process.

As we discussed earlier, real estate is not a particularly complex asset class when compared with the extreme uncertainty of venture capital and the unique strategic synergies involved with corporate M&A, both areas where I spent time earlier in my career. My old colleagues liked to refer to the real estate as "business-light". In those fields, relationships and corporate structures can create a situation where there is a naturally efficient buyer for deals. Of course, there are real opportunities for some real estate investors to add value through relationships, reputations, and operating efficiencies, but my experience is that the magnitude of those advantages are smaller than those on the corporate side.

So how can we use this reality to make better investment decisions? It is useful to understand that not all real estate investors are necessarily in the business of making the best (or least-worst, depending on market conditions) investment decisions, at least this is not their only concern. Many investors, particularly those in the institutional world, are in the business of avoiding investments that will look bad in retrospect. Being a successful long-term investment platform means being able to continue to consistently raise money. Doing bad deals that could plausibly have been good in retrospect is a forgivable offense by investors (the "nobody saw THAT coming!" defense), but doing bad deals that seemed crazy at the time is an unforgivable decision – something that could cost you a multi-billion account or kill your next fund. Regardless of the length of their track record, investment companies who can't raise their next fund or syndicate their next deal are out of business.

This tendency exists in other asset classes but is particularly strong in the real estate world, where investors' "hit rate" of successful deals is expected to be relatively high. In venture capital, a small percentage of deals are expected to be successful, making up for a majority of poor (as defined by their ex-post performance) deals. Still, the same factors exist in the VC world, creating inefficiencies in the market to be exploited by investors who are willing to focus on long-term performance at the risk of looking bad in the medium term. In a 2014 interview, Mark Andreessen of Andreessen Horowitz describes this as an important part of their strategy, and one reason why the biggest investment successes are rarely obvious in advance (Andreessen 2014).

To take advantage of inefficiently risk-averse investment decisions generally in the industry requires focusing on investments that are non-consensus, a.k.a. unpopular. Success requires that your risk-adjusted returns have to be the primary factor in your investment decisions, not your reputation. The following 2x2 matrix repurposes Andreessen's venture capital investment strategy to describe the range of investment possibilities in the real estate investment world:

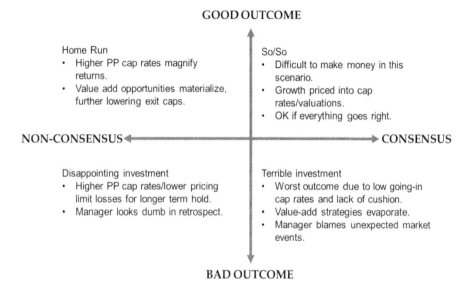

GOOD OUTCOME

Home Run
- Higher PP cap rates magnify returns.
- Value add opportunities materialize, further lowering exit caps.

So/So
- Difficult to make money in this scenario.
- Growth priced into cap rates/valuations.
- OK if everything goes right.

NON-CONSENSUS ←————————————————————→ **CONSENSUS**

Disappointing investment
- Higher PP cap rates/lower pricing limit losses for longer term hold.
- Manager looks dumb in retrospect.

Terrible investment
- Worst outcome due to low going-in cap rates and lack of cushion.
- Value-add strategies evaporate.
- Manager blames unexpected market events.

BAD OUTCOME

2X2 Real Estate Investment Outcome Matrix

On the right half of the matrix are consensus deals that "check all the boxes" for institutional investors when they are purchased; meaning they are in markets with strong economic prospects, the underlying real estate is new and well-built, and the locations are "main & main". All the market research supports strong rent growth projections. Everyone expects the market to do well and the real estate to perform well. Naturally, since these properties are an easy sell, competition is fierce for these deals and prices are bid up. Lenders provide aggressive (risky) loans, further fueling competition and making it more difficult to invest with a conservative capital structure.

If the market performs as expected (the top-right quadrant of the matrix), these consensus deals are so/so performers. The aggressive pricing when they were purchased makes it very hard to have an exceptionally good investment return on consensus deals since investors' optimistic beliefs are incorporated into their purchase price assumptions.

If things go poorly for the investment (the bottom-right quadrant of the matrix), consensus deals are exceptionally bad performers. Successful buyers often have to use aggressive debt capital structures, limiting downside protection and creating a destructive cycle of financial and operational distress at the property level. Many value-add deals are particularly hard hit because both the market growth and the value-add growth assumptions evaporate at the same time. The only consolation for the managers in these deals is that everyone expected them to do well so the results are more easily blamed on unexpected market movements, making it possible for salespeople to continue to raise money for the next fund in the series.

On the left half of the matrix are non-consensus deals. These properties are ugly ducklings for one reason or another. Perhaps they are in a market that just lost a major employer or is seeing anemic economic growth. Perhaps the properties are unusual in comparison to other recent trades, so pricing is hard to justify based on recent comparable sales; imagine a high-end distressed condo project in an area dominated by apartment or commercial properties. Whatever the reason, these deals have limited competition and more attractive pricing because many investors fear looking bad if they lose money on a deal with such an obvious risk or deficiency. Lenders also fear these deals for the same reason, so tend to be more conservative, limiting all buyers to a less risky capital structure and further limiting competition.

If the market performs badly or the obvious risks come to fruition on these non-consensus deals (the bottom-left quadrant of the matrix), they do badly. Although it depends on the deal, since they often have conservative capital structures and more modest investment assumptions, these deals tend to be more disappointing than catastrophic for investors. Higher purchase price cap rates and lower per-pound pricing limit the pain when the properties are ultimately liquidated, and conservative debt hopefully allows the deals to be held long enough to be bailed out by the next investment cycle. Managers of these deals feel stupid and are forced to have "I told you so" conversations with investors and industry colleagues, compounding the pain in their pocketbook with additional pain from the injury to their pride.

On the other hand, if these non-consensus deals do well (the top-left quadrant of the matrix), investors benefit from a near perfect storm of factors creating an exceptional deal. Long-tail market events far exceed conservative rent growth estimates and create the potential for selling deals as a value-add opportunity for the next buyer, which can significantly compress exit cap rates and increase sale values. Stronger markets support participation by a broader group of consensus investors, creating additional market liquidity and further driving up prices. Solving physical, environmental, or entitlement problems with a property can have the same effect. Stronger performance begets more aggressive financing for the ultimate buyer, supporting stronger pricing and further driving up returns.

Investors focused on achieving strong risk-adjusted returns are well served to target less popular non-consensus strategies with downside protection and the possibility to outperform if the market turns around or a functional problem with the property is solved. These deals tend to be scary, since the risks are obvious, but this is exactly why they outperform. Have courage, but don't forget to diversify.

Staying Power & Path Dependence

We discussed earlier the mechanics of real estate valuation, and how it leads the industry in general to underestimate volatility and risk. Taking that as a given, how do we incorporate this reality into a practical investment strategy in real estate?

Embrace the uncertainty. Real estate investing, like life, is messy, random, and frequently inexplicable. The tendency of most investors to underestimate this reality creates opportunities – some of the best acquisitions are from distressed sellers being forced to liquidate good real estate at a discount due to poor capitalization choices. Your primary goal as a long-term investor should be to avoid distress – don't blow up!

While there are some fundamentally bad real estate deals, many deals fall into distress due to timing. If a property can be held long enough, the market will often bail you out. This can admittedly take a long time in some cases, but there is real value in the capacity to be patient. On the other hand, if your property can't make debt service payments, you can expect the lender to foreclose and liquidate immediately (or impose strict penalties in a best-case scenario). If property values recover shortly thereafter, you're out of luck; you already took a complete loss.

Take the following example showing a hypothetical property's investment returns if purchased with lower leverage or with higher leverage:

Importance of Staying Power

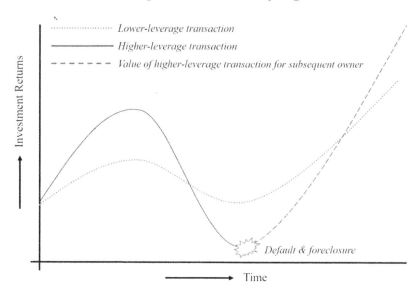

The lower leverage scenario suffers some volatility during the hold period but ends up with modest returns for investors. The higher leverage scenario does better initially but suffers more during the downturn, at which point the lender forecloses and the equity investors lose everything. Note that if the property could have been held long enough, the value would have recovered, and the equity investors would have done fine. This fact is irrelevant in practice. The lender, or subsequent owner of the property will benefit from any recovery in values, not the former owners.

This is of course not a quantitative example; it's meant to describe a common set of paths created by different investment strategies. As you can see, real estate investments tend to be path dependent and investment returns are defined not only by the purchase and sales prices of an asset, but by the operational profile and value of the asset during the hold period. Other types of investments can be similar - for stock investors, getting a margin call can mean being forced to liquidate investments at the worst possible time to repay debt. Looking for deals with a lower chance of forced liquidation will free up liquidity to re-invest during market downturns (the best investment opportunities), or at least make your sleep a little sounder when those downturns come.

Once you start viewing long term market forecasts and financial projections with suspicion and embracing the uncertainty inherent in the process, you are free to spend more time evaluating real estate based on some simpler, time tested metrics. The most important of these for long term investors are the lender metrics (such as the revenue stress test) described earlier. Rather than evaluating deals by looking for the highest pro forma returns, find a group of deals that have generally acceptable investment returns and pick your investment based on the fundamental quality of the real estate (building and location) and its ability to withstand downturns. If the market is strong, the upside will take care of itself. 15% IRR or a 17% IRR... does it really matter? When things take a turn south though, that slightly less risky deal could mean the difference between a 3% IRR over 10 years and a total loss in year 5. Keep in mind Nassim Nicholas Taleb's advice that "It does not matter how frequently something succeeds if failure is too costly to bear".

Another factor to keep in mind is the concept of long-term reversion to the mean. When real estate is going through a boom or a bust, it's easy to lose sight of the many cycles the sector has ridden out before. Like other investment classes, it's tempting to succumb to the "this time is different" mentality. But based on real estate's history, this time is very likely not different. This too shall pass. Simple math tells us that rents can't outpace income over the long term. If they did, they would eventually consume all of humankind's spending power. Likewise, if rents are too low to justify new construction, nothing will be built until rents recover. If rents are high enough to justify new construction, properties will be built until rents drop. Of course, with the impact of inflation, values and rents do go up in real dollars over time, but it's still helpful to look at values in historical context, particularly taking into account inflation, to get a sense of where we stand in a cycle. If values are far below prior peak and rents don't justify new construction, it's probably a good time to be a patient buyer. Long term investors should value basic economics over market momentum.

As John Maynard Keynes famously (although perhaps apocryphally) said, "The market can remain irrational longer than you can remain solvent." If you are investing steadily through real estate cycles and have staying power, you stand a good chance of living through the ill-timed deals with mediocre returns and making exceptional investments during periods of market opportunity.

Ultimately there is no single formula for making good real estate investments. Over the years I have had the pleasure of speaking with many successful industry veterans, each of whom has tallied many wins and losses. Some have a few more wins on the board, but all have taken some lumps from the market over the years. As you design your own bespoke real estate investment plan, keep your personal risk tolerance firmly in mind. Only you really know your own ability to withstand losses and your own motivation to spend the time necessary to create a well-crafted investment portfolio. Honesty about this will serve you well over the long term.

CHAPTER 10: PULLING THE TRIGGER: INVESTMENT PROCESS & TIMELINE

"Buy the ticket, take the ride...and if it occasionally gets a little heavier than what you had in mind, well...maybe chalk it off to forced conscious expansion: Tune in, freak out, get beaten." – Hunter S. Thompson, Fear and Loathing in Las Vegas

Now that we have covered the types of investment options, let's briefly summarize the mechanics and timeline of actually committing to a transaction. Because this varies somewhat by operator and transaction type, this summary applies primarily to syndicated partnerships.

Initial Review

Most equity offerings start with a phone call or an email with a high-level overview of the property and investment plan. Hopefully, this will be a warm call and you will already have reviewed and selected the operator as someone you trust and are planning to do business with. If you are being referred to the investment or are being contacted for the first time, don't be pressured into skipping your GP due diligence due to time constraints or a nearly-subscribed offering. It's better to miss a good investment than to lock your money up for many years without doing all your homework. There are plenty ways to lose money due to calculated or unforeseen risks without also taking unnecessary risk on the GP! Also, most of the highest quality operators and the best transactions are oversubscribed through existing investors, so you should ask yourself why the GP needs your investment, if this is in fact such a great deal. There may be good reasons, for instance the group is making a long-term push to expand their equity base or a deal is unusually large for them, but it is at least worth understanding. As John Bogle, founder of the Vanguard Group said, "Time is your friend; impulse is your enemy."

The initial marketing effort may be as short as a quick email describing the opportunity, or it may be accompanied by an attached "tear sheet" (1-2-page overview) or "pitch book" (more extensive presentation). Marketing materials will usually include general information about the transaction such as the price, terms, and timeline. It will also go through the property, location, and investment plan. Information about the LP deal terms and background information on the GP will be summarized as well.

At this point, the GP is usually trying to understand how much demand they have for the deal and get a preliminary list of investors and amounts so they can plan the rest of their equity raise. They will want to know, based on the quick profile of the deal, if you are interested.

Review the deal, decide if it fits in your investment plan, and provide honest feedback about your level of interest. At this point, you should have enough information to know generally if it works: Is it the right size investment? The right operator? Is the product type, strategy, and geography a fit? If you are not interested or on the fence, tell them so they can plan accordingly. Providing a preliminary commitment and pulling out of the deal later without a reasonable explanation is logistically annoying and won't land you on the top of the call list for the next deal from the same GP. If you are interested, keep in mind that at this point you haven't received enough information to commit to a deal.

Some operators will begin this preliminary equity raise immediately after they put a deal under contract and in parallel with their due diligence process. This is often the case with newer operators or larger deals, when the GP is out of their comfort zone or just wants to know that the equity has been raised before they risk non-refundable deposits. If this is the case, just make sure you have a chance to review all material findings from due diligence and understand the final loan terms before you need to fully commit to the deal.

Final Offering Package

When the time comes for final commitments, investors will receive a full offering package, which includes a standard set of legal and marketing documents.

The specific combination of documents in an offering can vary depending on the deal, operator, and legal structure, but here is a common set:

- Private Placement Memorandum (PPM)
- Limited Partnership Agreement (for LPs) or Operating Agreement (for LLCs)
- Subscription agreement
- Other related materials

Private Placement Memorandum (PPM)

The PPM is probably the single most important document to review. It serves two very important purposes:

1. Marketing: It describes why the deal is great and you should be absolutely begging for the opportunity to invest.
2. CYA: It describes every conceivable risk and why an investor would have to be insane to participate.

If those two purposes seem at completely at odds, they are. The goal of the PPM is to describe both the investment opportunity and risks. If the drawbacks and risks haven't been fully communicated to investors, those investors could sue the GP after the fact in an attempt to rescind their investment. As a result, PPMs are exceedingly conservative, sometimes humorously so, about disclosing potential risks. Having written many offerings, they still strike me as schizophrenic. One paragraph raves about the excellent prospects for job growth in the market and another includes a warning about the risk from uninsured damages caused by terrorist acts.

Not all PPMs are organized the same way, but they usually contain nearly all information relevant to your investment decision. They describe the real estate, the legal structure and deal terms, provide information about the GP background and compensation, and list investment risks. Each major issue addressed in this book should also be included in a thorough PPM.

Take note of the date on the cover. Think of this like the expiration date on a carton of milk; after this date passes the contents will become increasingly questionable. If you are reviewing an old offering, understand why it has not already been subscribed and ask what may have changed since the original offering date. This is true for both syndications and funds. It's common for funds to have lengthy offering processes, but you should still ask what has changed. In many cases, funds well into their offering process will have made first draws and purchased their first properties, giving you an initial indication of the assets you will be investing in.

As you go through the document, keep a running list of questions. Not all of these questions will necessarily be for the GP, you should also be noting any legal and tax issues that will need to be reviewed by your attorney or CPA. Make sure you are completely comfortable with the transaction before providing a commitment to invest.

Don't be one of the majority of investors who looks at the photos in the pitch books and skips everything else. The PPM can be incredibly boring (sometimes purposefully so), but it's worth pouring the extra cup of coffee, turning off your phone, and powering through it. Unlike some of the other transaction documents, the PPM is relatively coherent even without a J.D., and after you read a few they start to fall into a rhythm so you will know where to look for important terms.

Limited Partnership Agreement or Operating Agreement

This agreement defines the precise mechanics of the LP or LLC entity. Among many other things, it describes what can and can't be done with the entity, how decisions are made, investor classes, contributions and distributions, recordkeeping, provisions for replacement of the GP/Manager, and dispute resolution. Some of this is comprehensible to the layperson, some not. The most material terms in the LPA should be disclosed in the PPM but you can't necessarily count on this. A thorough review requires a qualified attorney.

Other Transaction Materials

Other deal related materials may be made available, often through an online portal for investors, with more detailed information about the transaction (rental studies, appraisals, engineering/environmental reports, surveys, and other internal or third party generated reports) or copies of relevant documents (such as purchase agreements, loan commitments, leases, etc.). These are provided as additional information to address specific investor questions/concerns and to demonstrate transparency to investors. If you are feeling diligent and have some spare time, read through these for a better understanding of the transaction. If the offering is well crafted however, all critical information from these documents and risks to the transaction should be incorporated into the PPM and other marketing materials.

Subscription Agreement

The subscription agreement describes the process for committing to the investment and submitting your funds. The actual commitment can be as short as a single page but is typically two or three. Each investor provides the investment amount, their name, vesting information, contact information, the type of organization making the investment, and direct deposit information for distributions.

Pay specific attention to how you choose to vest your investment, and make sure to consult your advisers as needed – is it coming from a taxable account, tax deferred retirement account, trust, or other entity? Is it made individually or jointly? This decision could have important tax consequences and you may not be able to change your mind later. Make sure your planned vesting is allowed and understand what paperwork needs to be completed to finalize it. As an example, investments from individual retirement accounts (IRAs) or other accounts administered by a third party, if they are even allowed, may be subject to additional administrative fees and take extra time for paperwork to be completed and submitted. They could require special permission and paperwork both by the GP and by your IRA administrator. You may need to start this process well in advance of making your actual cash contribution.

For investments with accreditation requirements, the GP will include a questionnaire that needs to be completed and returned. This questionnaire documents each investor's accreditation for the GP and is held on file for each investor.

Review and Commitment

At this point, if you are still serious about the deal, it's time to have the offering reviewed by your financial, tax, and legal advisers. The larger the investment you plan to make, the more important this review is. There are too many investor-specific issues to even attempt to address here, and you should rely on your advisers to know your individual situation to provide you with good advice. Obviously, this can be costly, and you need to decide for yourself the most efficient course of action based on your own personal situation.

If you decide to invest, fill out the subscription agreement, submit your funds (unless you are a fund investor and subject to periodic capital calls), and wait. To accommodate the fundraising process, the GP usually has a period (for instance 30 days) to decide whether the subscription is accepted or not. If it is accepted, the subscription agreement is countersigned and returned to you.

That's all there is to it. You're now along for the ride. Hang on and have fun.

CHAPTER 11: KEY TAKEAWAYS

For your consideration, I present you with the following summary suggestions for long-term investors in private real estate:

- Don't blow up. The next cycle can't bail you out if you don't make it through the downturn.
- Avoid crappy real estate.
- Read the PPM before you invest. Yes, it's tedious, but do it anyway. You won't regret it!
- Spread your bets. Like any investment, avoid concentration risk with one operator or product type.
- Boring is smart. Avoid high leverage and complicated deal structures meant primarily to juice returns.
- Invest with the best. High quality operators see the best opportunities and can negotiate the best deals.
- Keep the big picture in mind when evaluating fees and promotes.
- Pick non-consensus and un-loved strategies. The cyclical nature of real estate tends to reward contrarians more consistently than in other businesses.
- Approach market forecasts and financial models with a healthy dose of skepticism.
- Don't invest with jerks. Mostly because they tend to treat LPs badly when things go south, but also... why encourage them?
- Be honest about your tolerance for risk and your investment horizon. Once you are in there is no turning back.

POSTSCRIPT

I hope this book has provided you with a better understanding of the private real estate investment world and is a useful tool as you navigate the myriad investment options available to you. In the years since it was first released, the interest in this book has exceeded my wildest expectations. It has become course material in college classes, introductory reading for new employees in major corporations, and has generated a tremendous amount of feedback from readers all over the world. Watching my quixotic hobby reach such a broad audience has been incredibly satisfying, and is, I think, a testament to the inadequacy of information generally available to investors. An updated edition will at some point make sense given how quickly the real estate industry and capital markets are shifting. Although some market specifics may change, I hope the most important themes of this book (property quality, sponsor selection, and general conservatism) will stand the test of time. While writing this updated postscript from my home office during the COVID-19 crisis, they are certainly being put to the test!

As a self-published book, this tome did not benefit from the type of editorial review a traditionally published book would have received. While much of it is written based on personal experience, I also reached out to a variety of industry participants for additional information or feedback about concepts described herein (thank you to all of you, you know who you are!). In the event I missed something, you believe something in this book is factually incorrect or misleading, you have questions or suggestions about topics covered, or perhaps you just disagree with me, please contact me and let me know. I will do my best to correct material errors and make updates to the book if reasonably possible. I can't guarantee I will respond in a timely manner if I'm closing a deal, but would sincerely appreciate any feedback that would help me improve the quality of this book for future readers. If you are so compelled, feel free to reach out to me at prehandbook@gmail.com. Thank you to all of you who have reached out already to provide feedback, many of your comments have been incorporated in the current version of this book.

Because my use of a pseudonym makes book promotion somewhat challenging, I would truly appreciate a review of this book through www.amazon.com (or anywhere, really), which will help other people find it and provide me with feedback for improvements to future editions. Even better, if you found it entertaining and informative, please take a moment to recommend it to a few friends.

Thank you in advance and best of luck with all your endeavors, real estate and otherwise.

REFERENCES

Andreessen, Marc, interview by Russ Roberts. 2014. *Marc Andreessen on Venture Capital and the Digital Future* (May 19).

Davidson, Lee. 2005. "Politics and Policy: the Creation of the Resolution Trust Corporation." *FDIC Banking Review.*

Fama, Eugene F. 1991. "Efficient Capital Markets: II." *The Journal of Finance* 1.

Goodwin Procter. 2014. "REsource." *Goodwin Procter.* http://www.goodwinprocter.com/~/media/Files/Publications/Goodwin%20Procter%20Articles/REsource/2014/REsource_Fall2014.pdf.

Grossman, S. Ira. 2013. *Property Condition Reports: What do Investors Need?* National: GlobeSt.com.

Haughey, Rick. 2015. "Crowdfunding Grows Up." *NMHC.*

Mancuso, Leola Ross & John. 2011. *Structuring a private real estate portfolio.* Russell Investments.

massolution. 2015. "2015CF-RE Crowdfunding for Real Estate." Industry Report.

Moloney, James. 2015. "SEC Adopts Final Rules Implementing "Regulation A+"." *Harvard Law School Forum on Corporate Governance and Financial Regulation.*

Morrison Foerster. 2015. "Frequently Asked Questions About Real Estate Investment Trusts." *media.mofo.com.* Accessed October 18, 2015. http://media.mofo.com/files/Uploads/Images/FAQ_REIT.pdf.

NAREIT. n.d. *NAREIT.* Accessed October 27, 2015. www.reit.com.

Pedersen, Lasse. 2015. "Are Markets Efficient or Irrational? Actually, a Bit of Both." *Institutional Investor.*

PEI/PERE. 2012. *Understanding Private Real Estate.* London: PEI Media.

Real Property Association of Canada. 2008. "Private Equity Real Estate Funds: An Institutional Perspective."

Rekenthaler. 2015. "The Problem With Alternative Investing." *Morningstar*, June 6.

Toder, Eric. 2008. "Business Taxation: What are flow-through enterprises and how are they taxed?" *Tax Policy Center.* January 23. Accessed October 18, 2015. http://www.taxpolicycenter.org/briefing-book/key-elements/business/flow-through.cfm.

U.S. Internal Revenue Service. 2008. "Like Kind Exchanges Under IRC Code Section 1031." *IRS.gov.* February 18. Accessed October 18, 2015. https://www.irs.gov/uac/Like-Kind-Exchanges-Under-IRC-Code-Section-1031.

U.S. Securities & Exchange Commission. 2013. "Investor.gov." *Investor Bulletin: Accredited Investors.* September 23. Accessed October 18, 2015. http://www.investor.gov/news-alerts/investor-bulletins/investor-bulletin-accredited-investors.

Printed in Great Britain
by Amazon